BITTMAN
BREAD

BITTMAN BREAD

No-Knead Whole Grain Baking for Every Day

MARK BITTMAN AND KERRI CONAN

Photography by Jim Henkens

Houghton Mifflin Harcourt

BOSTON NEW YORK 2021

For information about permissions to reproduce selections from this book, write to
trade.permissions@hmhco.com or to Permissions, Houghton Mifflin Harcourt Publishing Company,
3 Park Avenue, 19th Floor, New York, New York 10016.

hmhbooks.com

Library of Congress Cataloging-in-Publication Data
Names: Bittman, Mark, author. | Conan, Kerri, author. | Henkens, Jim, illustrator.
Title: Bittman bread : no-knead whole grain baking for every day / Mark Bittman and Kerri Conan ;
photography by Jim Henkens.
Description: Boston : Houghton Mifflin Harcourt, 2021. | Includes index.
Identifiers: LCCN 2021018572 (print) | LCCN 2021018573 (ebook) | ISBN 9780358539339 (pob) |
ISBN 9780358539216 (ebk)
Subjects: LCSH: Cooking (Bread) | Bread. | LCGFT: Cookbooks.
Classification: LCC TX769 .B56 2021 (print) | LCC TX769 (ebook) | DDC 641.81/5—dc23
LC record available at https://lccn.loc.gov/2021018572
LC ebook record available at https://lccn.loc.gov/2021018573

Food styling by Callie Meyer
Book design by Toni Tajima

Printed in China
SCP 10 9 8 7 6 5 4 3 2 1

Contents

Acknowledgments

A few years back, when we started working together on naturally fermented whole grain bread, neither of us expected the road to lead to a book, or to involve so many people, pulling for us and willing to help.

Let's start by thanking our dearest who lived with us and our bowls of dough from day one. I (Mark) live with the brilliant and wonderful Kathleen Finlay, whose oohs and aahs and general appetite for life (as well as bread) keep me energized in many ways, including baking. The pandemic gave me the opportunity to drop breads on neighbors' porches and feel like I was doing some good—and most of them were kind enough to let me know that indeed, I was. My kids, Kate and Emma, showed me their appreciation by starting to bake their own, and feeding it to my fabulous sons-in-law, Jeffrey and Nick—and to my grandson, Holden, who clamored for "gumps" bread from the time he had teeth.

From me (Kerri), first big hugs out to my sister, Kat Conan, and niece, Kylie Jo Cagle. We toasted a lot of those early loaves together while we were caring for our beloved Anna Rae. I am grateful for you both every day and can't wait to pull another bag of bread from my suitcase for us to share. I am grateful that my wonderful longtime friends and extended family are far too numerous to name. Thank you one and all. And always, infinite love to my wildly imaginative husband, Sean Santoro, who unconditionally supports me during the important times between feeding the starter and batches of Crumby Cookies. With his inspiration, everything is possible.

We are fortunate to work with a team of wonderful colleagues, who are crucial to this and all other operations. Daniel Meyer, pizza and pretzel troubleshooter, sure, but mostly one of our supportive resident geniuses; Melissa McCart, editor, reporter, and writer extraordinaire of The

Bittman Project; and again big thanks to Kate Bittman, who miraculously somehow manages to combine exceptional content generation *and* promotion. And to Danielle Svetcov, our agent, welcome aboard! She helped us develop the right concept and proposal and then get the book into the right hands.

We're so lucky those hands belong to our longtime publisher Houghton Mifflin Harcourt. Thank you to everyone who touched this book along the way: Stephanie Fletcher, Deb Brody, Karen Murgolo, Melissa Lotfy, Rebecca Springer, Kim Kiefer, Toni Tajima, Suzanne Fass, Andrea DeWerd, Katie Tull, and Shara Alexander.

Jim Henkens brought each recipe and visual cue to life and light with his stunning photography, helped with the baking, and travelled across the country to capture two authors in action. Kerri and Jim were fortunate to work with food stylist Callie Meyer in Seattle—just the three of us! She lived this project, too, and it shows.

Then there are the grain experts and bakers—professional and home enthusiasts—who tested recipes, shared equipment, and answered questions. I (Mark) want to single out especially my friends Bob Klein from Community Grains and Rick Easton of Bread & Salt, as well as Sam Fromartz and Ellen King, who did more to get me on the right track then either of them know. Drs. Stephen Jones of Washington State University Breadlab and Andrew Ross at Oregon State; Jerilyn Brusseau; Kevin Morse (and everyone at Cairnspring Mills); Jim Challenger of Challenger Breadware; the generous folks at Emile Henry; Danny and Judy Kramer; Gina and Dan Glynn; Julie Gottesman; Corissa Cox; Carrie Kartman; and Cassidy Stockton (and her colleagues) at Bob's Red Mill. And a special shout-out to Lodge for making "the pot."

There's good reason bakers have been essential to villages, neighborhoods, and households throughout history. We hope this book helps you be that person for the people in your life.

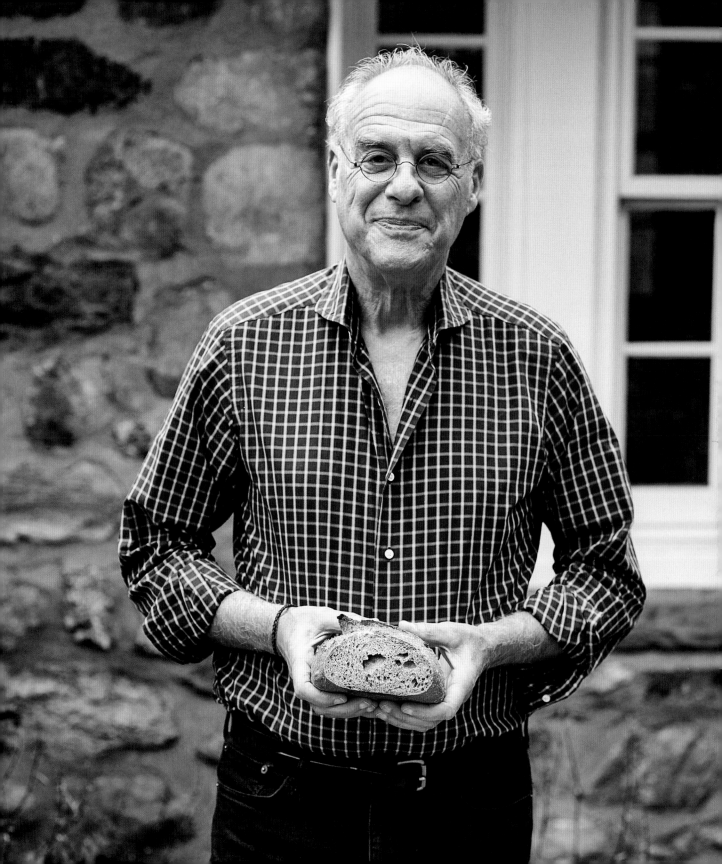

Introduction

THE JOURNEY TO WHOLE GRAIN BAKING

Among the do-it-yourself projects of the early days of the COVID-19 pandemic was a widespread obsession with bread baking. There were many reasons for this: People had time on their hands; bread baking is soothing (and habit forming!); most bakeries were shuttered, at least temporarily; and mutually supportive communities developed. Then there was the discovery that the quality of the new bakers' bread was better than whatever they'd been buying.

By that time my coauthor Kerri Conan and I were hard at work on this book. We believed (and still do) that we'd made a series of discoveries around whole grain bread baking that would make it more accessible to more home cooks than it had been in a century.

I'd spent about fifty years baking bread (since September 1970), some seriously. I started with white bread loaves using the *Joy of Cooking* recipe and took it from there—James Beard, Bernard Clayton, Laurel Robertson, Tassajara—the seventies classics, really.

In the early eighties my Connecticut friend Charlie van Over developed a food processor technique soon after that machine became popular, and I rode with that for quite some time. It made kneading by hand unnecessary (the machine did it for you) and produced excellent white flour baguettes. Trips to Italy and France influenced and inspired me, but I remained an occasional baker—someone who cooked a lot and considered bread a part of my repertoire, but I'd go weeks or months at a time without making bread.

In 2006, Jim Lahey of New York City's Sullivan Street Bakery called me at the *New York Times*. "I have a way to make bread, really good bread, with no kneading," he said. "Wanna see?" I said, "The food processor killed kneading ages ago." He said, "This bread is better than that."

Knowing that there's always room for improvement, I went to visit Jim at his Hell's Kitchen location and, because the *Times* was getting into video, brought a recording team with me. Jim is generous, patient, smart, a terrific baker, and a wonderful human. We had fun, my jaw dropped, and the *Times* published Jim's recipe for the now-famous No-Knead Bread, shared millions of times since then, and a touchstone during the recent baking craze.

Indeed, Jim's dough requires no kneading, using time instead of work to develop strength and elasticity. Equally important was Jim's reintroduction of the old and brilliant technique of baking *en cloche*—that is, baking the dough first in a closed environment like a Dutch oven—to enhance moistness and maximize rising, then removing the cover so the crust sets. (Professionals have hearth ovens that inject steam, and it's the home baker's job to try to mimic that. A covered pot is the best technique anyone's come up with, and our recipe goes one step further to brown and crisp the nearly finished loaf directly on an oven rack.)

Jim's no-knead loaf is, for sure, the best white bread with the least amount of work and skill required of the home baker. It's not surprising that it has millions of enthusiasts.

But I wanted more. I wanted an excellent 100 percent whole grain loaf.

In 2015 I relocated to Berkeley and, living alone and with some time on my hands (I'd left the *Times* and was between book projects), I began taking bread more seriously. I was determined to leave white flour behind and, luckily, I'd met and befriended Bob Klein of Community Grains in Oakland. Bob was working with wheat farmers from California and the Pacific Northwest to find older strains of wheat that could simply be ground, without sifting or otherwise removing the bran or germ, to make good, truly whole grain bread.

As it turns out, making the best bread mostly means two things: mastering natural starter—usually called "sourdough," though it's not necessarily sour—and using real whole grains.

I say "real" whole grains because there are a lot of foods out there that call themselves "whole grain" that are not. If you take anything out, it's obviously no longer whole. A whole grain flour should have the same composition as the grain from which it was ground, as you'll see in Chapter 2, "The Why (and How) of Whole Grain Baking."

Many serious bakers—me included—don't believe you can bake really good whole grain bread without natural starter. Put another way: Commercial yeast (made possible by the nineteenth-century work of Louis Pasteur) cannot produce a satisfying whole grain bread.

The new home bakers have figured out the appeal of bread baking as relaxing, habit forming, fun, and something to show off on social media. All of that is true with bread made with white flour, so the question is, "Why make whole grain bread?"

My answer is: "It's better." When you update an old-fashioned technique and combine it with old-fashioned grain (again, whole), you can make the best bread you've ever had—and by best, I mean not only healthiest but far fuller tasting and more complex and satisfying than what you're (probably) used to. Naturally fermented whole grain bread is the bread that was long called "the staff of life," and the only bread I find worthy of that name.

Ancient and even preindustrial loaves were composed primarily of fermented whole grain—whether wheat or one of its ancestors like einkorn or emmer, or barley or rye—water, and salt. Those breads provided protein, fat, fiber, and a host of micronutrients. With a little dairy or meat or legumes and the occasional fresh fruit or vegetable, they formed the foundation of a solid diet that could support good health.

White bread can't do that. What it can do is be reproduced uniformly and cheaply; it can also be industrially sliced and loaded with preservatives. It can even be called "wheat bread" (which of course it is), but it can never be truthfully called "whole grain," because its flour has been stripped of the bran and grain, the key sources of nutrients in wheat.

Bread made only with white flour, or even some small portion of whole grain wheat flour, doesn't provide much in the way of nutrition. (That's why most packaged bread is fortified with added vitamins.) In fact, your digestive system treats it more like sugar than it does like ground whole wheat.

The convenience of white bread was a boon to wheat growers and especially processors in turn-of-the-twentieth-century America, and the shelf-stable stuff was gobbled up by city dwellers who, as factory and office workers, no longer had the time— or place, or energy, or even ingredients—to bake real bread. Rural people held out for as long as they could against factory bread and continued to bake, or at least buy at a local bakery, where whole grain bread remained the standard well into the twentieth century.

But those traditions are now pretty much gone, even in England, France, Germany, India, Italy, Turkey, and other places where wheat has long been important and where whole grain breads remained the standard until a couple of generations ago. (The dense ryes of northern Europe, corn tortillas, and Ethiopian injera made from teff are among the remaining exceptions.)

Those traditions are now being revived, for both long- and short-term reasons. The long-term reason is that good bread is actually good for you; it's not one of those carbs that you're often warned against. It also reminds you how simple nourishing food can be.

The short-term reason is that real whole grain bread is actually easy to make at home, needing only a little active time (and, yes, a lot of passive time), our technique, and an oven. You'll need a minimum of equipment, too, and of course some flour, but we can easily teach you the practice starting now.

When I began to make this kind of bread, six years ago as of this writing, I went through all of the machinations other people recommended to make sourdough starter (which we're going to mostly call, simply, "starter"). I won't bore you with the details of my experiments right now, except to say that once I recognized what starter actually is—a friendly environment to cultivate the wild yeasts that live all around us—the answer became simple: Prime the pump with a little bit of store-bought yeast, and let it evolve. The process of making a starter takes a few days, but very little work.

This book begins with an improved version of the original no-knead bread, one whose purpose (other than to produce a loaf of bread!) is to introduce you to some of the handling techniques we use to make whole grain bread and to give you a live piece of dough that you can quickly and reliably turn into a natural starter, one that will live and thrive as you use it (or at least feed it) every now and then.

When I got much of this approach right, about three years ago, I was hooked: I'd mostly left white flour behind and combined many of the insights I'd learned over the years to bake a pretty good whole grain bread.

My results, however, were inconsistent, my techniques too complicated to communicate easily, and my breads just weren't as good as I knew they could be. I talked to (and baked with) better bakers— Sam Fromartz in Washington, DC, Ellen King in Chicago, Rick Easton in Pittsburgh and later Jersey City, a few of the Bay Area people focusing on whole grain bread (the people in what I think of as the Bob Klein crowd), Steve Jones at the Washington State University Breadlab—and I learned a lot. But with the exception of Sam (whose book *In Search of the Perfect Loaf* is brilliant), all of these people were professionals; they weren't focusing on teaching home cooks how to make a great bread. (This doesn't mean I'm not thankful or in their debt; I am.)

I needed to get to a place where I could produce great bread any time I wanted to, and to be able to offer you the ability to do the same thing. That's what I do, after all: I learn how to cook something and try to make it so that you can do it as well as I—or better. And over the years, increasingly key to that process was the involvement of my long-time collaborator (we are closing in on twenty years!), Kerri Conan.

Kerri combines genius and determination like no one else, and we work well together. I'm intuitive, hard working, and a little flaky; she is thoughtful with laser focus, hard working, and also a little flaky.

We had met in 1990 in New York, where she was a cookbook editor. When we started this project, Kerri lived in Kansas; she now lives in Washington State, so this, like all of our collaborations, has been done by phone, email, text, photo, live video, whatever. (COVID-19 had no impact on our

collaboration, except we sadly could not unite to produce photos.)

We began talking about bread and baking almost every day. We experimented with all sorts of flours, from super-commercial (I made, not long ago, an excellent loaf with some ShopRite whole wheat flour I found in a freezer) to home-milled grains, to flour sent to us by farmers and millers and marketers all over the country. We've tinkered with nearly every conceivable variable: We've slowed the process down to make it more leisurely and sped it up so we weren't as bound to the kitchen. We've used a variety of nonwheat grains and other ingredients. We've tinkered like mad with ratios and timing, almost always relying on the bare minimum ingredients: starter, flour, water, and salt.

Here's our process: You make starter. You use that starter to make what we call a "jumpstarter"—a mixture of starter, flour, and water—that sits overnight (or through the day), and ensures uniform, consistent rising power. You add more flour and water to the jumpstarter to produce dough; that sits for a while. You add salt and maybe flavoring, or seeds, or walnuts, whatever. (I'm just talking about the basic bread here; this book includes many variations and spins, of course.) You let it sit for a while, then you fold it four times, with more sitting time in between. Finally, you shape it and bake it in a covered pot lined with parchment paper.

Do that, and you will have produced a 100 percent whole grain bread that is probably unlike any you've ever tasted before, let alone made.

Our process can be done on your schedule, with almost any timing you like, even if you work nine to five. It will not fail you. And it will give you a product that is superior from every perspective: taste, texture, healthfulness, resource use. Our guess is that as you make our bread, your consumption of white bread will shrink until it approaches zero. Ours has.

Prepare for your own journey: Your first bread may have you scratching your head, and it certainly won't be as good as your tenth, and that one won't be as good as your fiftieth, but by then your bread will be as beautiful as the ones you see on these pages, and you will produce that level of bread whenever you want to. You will be transformed, I swear.

And when you master the process (months ago, I finally said to Kerri, "This is getting too easy!" so we started working on other baked foods)—and you will—your breads will be consistently fabulous. Not one of the hundreds of loaves Kerri and I have baked following this method has been anything but a winner, and they're all better than anything we can buy in a store. I'll go further: Unless you live near a bakery owned by people who really care (like those I mentioned above), you are not going to find a way to get better bread into your life.

Starting is easy, and you'll see that what we offer here is more than a series of recipes, but really a gradual understanding of a process that will allow you have fun and even grow personally (you'll certainly become more patient and intuitive) while making consistently outstanding whole grain bread a part of your cooking routine. Meanwhile, whether you bake daily, weekly, or now and then, you'll be nourishing yourself and others and exploring a fascinating mystery that was first discovered more than 10,000 years ago.

From this point on, my solo voice will (mostly) disappear. After Kerri steps in to tell her bread history, the narrative picks up with the two of us speaking in one joint first person plural voice, augmented by a couple of dialogues. First, let's hear from Kerri . . .

Until Mark and I decided to take this journey together, my bread baking experience was yeasted and spotty. In 1987 I became assistant to cookbook editor Carole Lalli at Simon and Schuster. Though I wasn't professionally trained, my home-cooking background was rock solid and included a wide range of desserts. Since the age of six, I had prepared everyday and holiday meals with my mom, a home economics teacher with a keen interest in entertaining and restaurant-style projects. But she wasn't that big on yeasted baking. Other than the glazed fruit–stuffed yule loaves she gifted at Christmas and a sourdough starter she took for a brief dance in the early 1970s, she remained focused on cookies. Bread was the one food category I didn't learn at her elbow.

Carole immediately pointed me to Bernard Clayton's *New Complete Book of Breads* and his chapter and recipe, "The First Loaf." (When I opened to that page to confirm the title, a small card with my faded shopping list tumbled out. Awwww!)

Over the years I baked a little from Bernie's book, and bought a couple of others. Later, as a freelancer, I occasionally had to test this bread or that one. Developing a brioche-style cinnamon roll for a Williams Sonoma book became a turning point in deciding to bake more regularly.

By the time my husband and I moved to rural Kansas and I started working with Mark, my repertoire had expanded to half–whole wheat pizza dough and an everyday sandwich loaf—both yeasted and somewhat dense. Like everyone else, I latched on to Mark and Jim Lahey's no-knead bread. My other breads were functional, not special. Maintaining a starter seemed onerous and a little scary. But unlike Mark, no-knead was enough for me.

That is, until he invited me—no, challenged me—to try his lump-of-dough starter and join him in the quest for a doable whole grain loaf. Funny how easy his sourdough approach was. I enthusiastically joined the quest.

As Mark knows, part of our success is the way we work together, pushing each other to try new things to make the bread more accessible—and better. We sent thousands of texts, emails, and photos back and forth over the years. And it's certainly true that we complemented each other in our interests and expertise. While we did consult with scientists and scholarly publications, he and I experimented and communicated in a way that was always more playful than scientific. After all, we were just cooking.

The result is this book, which unfolds in six progressive chapters: Making your starter and a first loaf; a detailed discussion of grains, flours, equipment, and timing; feeding the starter and producing your first "Bittman Bread"; other loaves in the same vein, but wildly varied; pizza and flatbread and rolls and savory pancakes; sweet things including pancakes and waffles.

Our goal is lofty but simple: We want to make naturally leavened whole grain bread the centerpiece of nutritious meals.

START
WITH
STARTER

CHAPTER 1

AND BAKE A BEGINNER LOAF

Learn the Bittman Bread technique with this spin on no-knead bread

I T'S ME, KERRI, getting the story rolling. A few years ago, I asked Mark what I thought was a simple question: "Which recipe should I use for making a sourdough starter?" Until then, I'd only made yeasted breads, but I knew that Mark had been on a naturally fermented bread binge, and that he was keen on working with whole grain doughs.

I wanted in on the action.

His answer was typical, if surprising: "You don't really need a recipe. Just make a no-knead bread, pull off a lump of dough halfway through, and start feeding it flour and water."

Thinking *This can't be right; it's too easy*, I spent (I would now say wasted) a day researching other, far more complicated and intimidating methods before following Mark's lead.

And here we are, almost four years later. He wanted to perfect and expand his whole grain sourdough method, and I was hankering for something new. Just about everything about our methods has changed since then—except starting the starter.

A starter is a mix of flour and water in which wild yeasts thrive. Some people call it "sourdough" or a "mother." The simplest way to start your starter is to get a blob or a jarful from someone else. If that's an option, do it. It doesn't matter if their starter is white, or rye, or whole wheat. It doesn't matter if it's old, or young. It just matters that it's alive. And you'll make it *your* starter in no time. (If you already have starter, skip all of this, and skip the Beginner Bittman Bread as well; go straight to Chapter 2, "The Why (and How) of Whole Grain Baking" on page 28.)

There are a number of interesting old-fashioned methods for creating starter—letting potatoes, fruit, or other food ferment, then using that to "sour" bread dough to create a yeast-friendly environment, or just making a flour-water mixture that will (hopefully) capture wild yeast and good bacteria. But these methods are tricky: Sometimes they work, and sometimes they don't. And even when they do, they take many days and frequent attention.

Our way is based on another tradition, that of using a piece of today's already-fermented dough as the basis for tomorrow's bread. Before the invention of commercial yeast, bakers would simply hold back a chunk of dough before baking and combine it with new flour and water to begin the process of creating the next loaf. As long as they made bread every day, there was no need to maintain a separate starter. We bake a lot of bread, but even we don't bake every day. So we needed a starter we could keep in our fridge, always ready to begin our next bread, even if we hadn't baked for a week.

Our little system works perfectly, and with our foolproof and super-fast starter-from-scratch recipe (easier than making a cup of coffee!), you'll be baking naturally fermented whole wheat bread three days after you start the process. After that, you'll only feed it when you bake, or at least once a week.

These are the broad strokes of making our starter: Use any white flour and dry yeast to prepare a loaf of Beginner Bittman Bread, essentially using the original no-knead bread technique. While making this first loaf, you'll reserve a bit of the dough, the foundation of your starter for all future loaves. (And you'll bake a loaf to enjoy.) The reserved lump of dough goes into a container to be fed a bit of flour and water over the next few days. By day 3, you'll have a full-fledged starter and be ready to bake whole grain Bittman Bread (page 55)—or any of the other recipes in the book.

Combining the minimal handling and slow fermentation approach of no-knead bread with what we have learned working with whole wheat serves three purposes: It gets your starter going, introduces the mixing and folding methods you'll use throughout this book, and lets you discover the simplicity and ease of our process.

Purists may complain that using commercial yeast in a sourdough starter is cheating. Indeed, there are differences between packaged yeasts and the wild (or ambient) strains you capture by letting flour and/or other ingredients ferment on their own. But your starter will quickly be populated by a combination of wild yeasts that's unique to your own environment, without any effort on your part besides feeding it. Don't think of it as a cheat but as a solid shortcut.

Beginner Bittman Bread, Plus Starting the Starter

This may be your first yeasted white loaf, but we predict it'll be your last, as you begin your journey into traditional baking. In this recipe, you'll get all the experience you need to create a starter and make a big leap toward the world of spectacular whole grain loaves and other naturally leavened foods. For the beginner bread, we're giving measurements in volume. After that we'll assume you use a scale. (You can always consult "Converting Weight to Volume" on page 43.)

And if you don't have a 2-quart pot yet, see "The Pot" on page 41 for some options. And remember, you can always save leftovers for one of the ideas starting on page 113, or Crumby Cookies on page 225.

The variations that follow serve two purposes: You can use them to make additional yeasted breads whenever you like. Or you can choose one of them as the recipe for your first starter or to begin another starter if you ever need a replacement or an extra.

Makes

1 loaf (12 to 14 ½-inch slices) and the base for the starter

Time

12 to 18 hours to mix, ferment, and bake the bread

3 days for the starter to get going, including a couple of hours intermittent attention

INGREDIENTS

2¾ cups all-purpose or bread flour, plus more for dusting

¾ teaspoon instant yeast, rapid rise yeast, or active dry yeast (it doesn't matter)

⅔ cup water, plus another ½ cup, and more as needed

1 teaspoon salt

Mix the bread dough

1. Put 1 cup of the flour and the yeast in a large bowl; add ⅔ cup water. Stir with a rubber spatula or large spoon until combined; the mixture will be loose and almost soupy. (This is what we call "jumpstarter.") Cover the bowl with plastic or a damp kitchen towel and let it sit at room temperature overnight, for at least 8 but no more than 12 hours. The jumpstarter will form bubbles.

2. Add the remaining 1¾ cups flour and ½ cup water. Use the spatula or spoon to gradually mix the water and flour into the dough. If necessary, add a few drops more water to integrate all of the flour; there should be no loose flour remaining in the bowl. The dough should be wet and sticky, but not nearly as runny as the jumpstarter. Continue to mix until you can use the spatula or spoon to shape the dough into a loose ball in the bowl. The texture will be shaggy, not smooth, but again, all flour should have been incorporated. Re-cover the bowl (dampen the towel again if necessary) and let it sit for an hour.

Start the starter

3. Remove about ½ cup of the dough and put it in a 1-quart jar or other airtight container; that will become your starter. (Make sure the container is at least double the size that you think you need, since the starter will expand as it sits. Also, you'll need room to mix in the flour and water in this container when you feed it later.) Cover the container loosely and let it sit at room temperature until you're ready to make the Bittman Bread Whole Wheat Starter (see the recipe on page 24).

continued →

Continue with the bread

4. Sprinkle the top of the remaining dough with the salt. Wet your hands (it helps to have a bowl of water nearby or to work near a faucet) and gather the dough into a ball, working it in your hands or pressing it in the bowl until it feels uniform and there are no lumps. (You'll feel when it's ready.) Cover it again and let it sit 30 minutes.

5. Now you will fold the dough at half-hour intervals (give or take). You can do this in the bowl if yours has a broad bottom (as pictured here) or on a cutting board or clean work surface as shown on page 66. Wet your hands and press the dough into a rough rectangle—don't murder it, just press it out flat. Then fold it over itself in thirds, like a letter. (Precision isn't important and aggressiveness doesn't help.) Repeat pressing and folding once or twice more, then fold the dough loosely over itself to gather and tuck it into a ball again. (See the photos on pages 65–69.) Use as much water on your hands and in the bowl (or on the cutting board or surface) as you need to—as much as the dough can absorb without creating a puddle. This technique is one fold. Cover the dough and let it sit for about 30 minutes.

6. Repeat the folds in Step 5 three more times. The dough will change every fold and become airier, more elastic—more beautiful, really. After the third fold (or whenever you have a minute), line a 2-quart ovenproof pot with a lid with a sheet of parchment paper that's big enough to overhang the rim by a few inches; press it into the bottom and crease the edges over the lip to keep it in place. (For other alternatives to "the pot," see page 41.) Make sure there's a rack in the middle of your oven with lots of space above it.

continued →

Beginner Bread dough after mixing in salt: It looks a little webby and might reveal early bubbles, but the dough is still lacking much structure, so it won't hold a shape.

Starting your starter: Find a container big enough for your lump of dough to grow. It should have a lid that either sits on top securely or screws down tight.

Beginner Bread dough after four folds: As the dough develops it becomes stretchier and stronger (more elastic without breaking). The bubbles should be getting bigger, too, but if you can't see them don't worry.

Beginner Bread, ready for the oven: After dusting with flour (or not) and slashing with an "X" (or some other pattern), it's time to cover the pot and pop the bread in the oven.

7. After the fourth fold, the dough ball will be a little more structured than before; use wet hands to tuck the edges underneath and smooth the bottom seam a bit. (Don't obsess over this.) Wet your hands once again, scoop the ball up from the bottom, and put it in the parchment paper–lined pot. Cover with the lid and let the dough rest until it puffs slightly, 10 to 20 minutes. Dust the top lightly with flour and cut a large *X* across the top of the loaf with a razor blade or sharp kitchen scissors. (It doesn't have to be an *X*—you can slash any design you like.) Replace the lid and put the pot in the middle of a cold oven. (Yes. *Cold*. That's not a typo.)

8. Set the oven to 485°F and bake undisturbed for 30 minutes. Remove the cover (the bread will have risen dramatically and will be golden and domed) and bake 15 minutes more. Turn the heat down to 400°F. Remove the pot from the oven; carefully remove the bread from the pot, peel off the parchment, and put the bread directly on the rack (mitts or a big spatula are handy here). Bake until the color of the crust is good and dark, 15 to 30 minutes more. (An instant-read thermometer inserted into the center should register about 205°F.) Transfer the bread to a wire rack to cool completely—this will take at least a couple of hours—before slicing.

continued →

Beginner Bittman No-Knead Olive Bread

If you already started your starter and just want to make this bread, remember to remove and discard ½ cup dough in Step 3 so the dough won't be too big for the pot. When you add the salt in Step 4, fold in up to ⅔ cup torn or chopped pitted black olives. If you'd like a little rosemary flavor, strip 1 or 2 sprigs, chop the leaves, and add them at the same time.

Beginner Bittman No-Knead Country Bread

When you mix the dough in Step 2, replace 1⅓ cups of the flour with whole wheat flour. If you already started your starter and just want to make this bread, remember to remove and discard ½ cup dough in Step 3 so the dough won't be too big for the pot.

Beginner Bittman No-Knead Rolls

After completing the fourth fold, grease a baking sheet generously with olive oil or softened butter. With wet hands, divide the dough into 8 pieces (or 10 pieces if you didn't reserve any dough to make a starter in Step 3). Gently roll the pieces into balls (they're better if they're not perfect) and put them on the prepared pan. Cut a small slash on top of each; just nick the dough. Put the pan in the cold oven and set the heat to 375°F. Bake until the rolls split and an instant-read thermometer stuck into the thickest part of one registers 200°F. Cool on a wire rack; eat warm if possible.

Beginner Bittman No-Knead Flatbread

Even if you already have starter, there's no need to remove the ½ cup dough in Step 3—you'll just have a slightly thicker flatbread. After the fourth fold, put a piece of parchment paper on a large, rimmed baking sheet and grease the parchment with 2 tablespoons olive oil. With wet hands, stretch the dough in the air as thinly as you can without tearing it, then put it in the pan and press it into an irregular rectangle about ¼ inch thick. Dab the top with more oil if you like and sprinkle with sea salt or a dusting of spice (like dried red chiles or black pepper or smoked paprika). Put the pan in the cold oven and set the heat to 400°F. Bake until crisp on the top and bottom but still a little spongy when you press on it, 15 to 20 minutes. Lift the flatbread from the pan, peel off the parchment, and cool on a wire rack. This is one bread that you can slice while it's still a little warm.

Bittman Bread Whole Wheat Starter

Here's how to make starter out of that lump of dough you set aside in Step 3 of the Beginner Bittman Bread recipe on page 16. White flour is okay if that's all you have, but put whole wheat flour on your shopping list so you can move on to the other recipes in this book.

Makes

Enough starter for any recipe in this book

Time

Less than a few minutes over the course of 3 days to get the starter going

INGREDIENTS

½ cup dough reserved from Beginner Bittman Bread (page 16)

1 cup water, plus more if needed

1 cup whole wheat flour, plus more as needed (white flour is okay; see the headnote)

1. To the lump of dough in its container, add ⅓ cup of the water and ⅓ cup of the whole wheat flour and stir until uniformly mixed. You want the starter loose enough to plop easily from a spoon, like a thick batter (see the photos on page 95). Add a little more water if necessary and stir—or shake—to combine. Let it sit at room temperature for 12 to 24 hours, loosely covered with plastic or a damp kitchen towel.

2. Repeat the feeding directions above twice more. If the starter crowds the container, remove some before adding the water and flour. (Use it to make pancakes, page 203. Or discard it—generally speaking something we frown upon, but in this instance it's okay.) After the third round

continued →

Feeding your starter the first time: The ratio of flour, water, and starter will be almost the same at the beginning.

Signs of life: After feeding and stirring, your starter will demonstrate it's active by bubbling and expanding, especially since it's at room temperature.

of feeding your starter, you're ready to make naturally fermented bread and replenish the starter (see the Bittman Bread recipe on page 55). Or you can wait up to 72 hours; just cover and refrigerate it until you need it.

From this point on, your starter will live in the fridge. Every time you bake—or once a week if you're not baking anything—you'll feed the starter equal weights of flour and water to compensate for whatever you use. Occasionally you may add a little more water to keep the starter loose enough to easily spoon or pour. (For more detail on this process, head to page 90.)

(opposite) Adding whole wheat flour: As soon as you can, feed the starter with whole wheat flour. After stirring, if it threatens to overflow the jar, discard ½ cup or so before the next feeding.

Say goodbye to white flour (top) and hello to whole grain rye, medium-grind cornmeal, and whole wheat flour.

CHAPTER 2

THE WHY (AND HOW) OF WHOLE GRAIN BAKING

Some science, the ingredients you'll use, and the tools you'll need

I F YOU'VE BAKED YOUR BEGINNER LOAF and are eager to head straight to Bittman Bread, go for it. As long as you've got starter, whole wheat flour, a scale, your 2-quart pot (or a workable alternative), and parchment paper, head over to page 55. Although you can bake any of the recipes in this book without becoming a bread nerd, and bake them well, at some point you may want to read the material that follows.

In this chapter, we've bundled the discussion of grain basics, fermentation, wheat flour, and home milling together, along with enough science to make the case for baking with whole grains and explain why our methods work so well. A second section covers all of the ingredients we use (other than whole wheat flour); finally we list the essential pots, pans, and tools you need. There's also a glossary and a few other bits for quick reference.

The Case for Whole Grains and Flours

Once you've baked and enjoyed a loaf of Beginner Bittman Bread, we encourage you to switch from white flour to whole grain and try other whole grain baked goods. (Actually, we almost insist.) That's a big change for many people, which is why we want to explain the elements that support excellent whole grain baking.

ANATOMY OF A GRAIN

To understand flour made from wheat, rye, rice, and other whole grains—essentially the seeds of different grasses—let's work from the outside in. The first task is done at the mill, and involves removing the inedible casing known as the hull, coating, or chaff from around the seed. With most cultivated wheats, this layer is papery and relatively easy to remove; for other grains like barley and the ancestors of wheat like spelt and einkorn, the hull may be so hard it must be buffed away. Until recently, the hulling process took away too much of the outer seed, leaving a not-quite-whole pearled grain, like the common ivory-colored barley, or farro. Fortunately there's now gentler milling technology that doesn't mess with the insides.

What remains is the edible seed—generally, this is considered the "whole grain." (It's commonly referred to as a "kernel" or "berry.") Of this, the remaining outside layer, which is fibrous and of varying shades of brown or green, is the bran; it's rich in vitamins and minerals, oils, protein, carbohydrates, and of course the all-important fiber, of which almost none of us gets enough. At the center of each seed is the reproductive part: the golden-colored germ, also rich in nutrients and oil. Together these two components of a whole grain give the berry much of its nutrition, fat, and flavor.

The rest of the berry—the majority, by weight—is the endosperm, which contains mostly carbohydrates and some protein. White flour is made of only endosperm, and keeps virtually forever, because without the oils of the bran and germ, there's little left to spoil.

White flour is easy to bake with and produces incomparably light breads and pastries. It's also nutritionally bereft, a near-perfect delivery system for empty calories. There is a place for it, but not as a dietary staple. That's because the body digests white flour the same way it does sugar: fast and furious. Stripped of fiber and most of its nutrients, white flour is metabolized quickly, delivering almost all of its energy in one fell swoop rather than the slow and sustained nutrition from whole foods.

You probably know much of this: Whole grains are absolutely better for you than those stripped of nutrients; from a health perspective, if you choose refined grains you may as well be eating fast food. That's why we're throwing white flour under the bus.

The obvious challenge is that the whole wheat counterparts of most baked goods always seem to fall short. We're here to remedy that, at least in part. There is precisely one recipe and one variation in this book that use white flour, and our goal is that you use it to make starter, then kiss white-flour bread goodbye. All of the other breads and treats use whole grain (mostly wheat) exclusively, and we guarantee that you will love them.

THE IMPORTANCE OF NATURAL FERMENTATION

After baking for well over a combined 75 years, we can assert with absolute confidence that the key to delicious baking with 100 percent whole grains is to begin with a naturally fermented starter. It's difficult to produce even a pretty good loaf with commercial yeast; it's impossible to produce a great one. Yet with a natural starter—sourdough—baking superb whole grain breads and pastries is easy.

Let us explain.

As dough sits, whatever yeast is present converts the carbohydrates in flour to gas in a process known as fermentation. This can happen anywhere between 40° and 120°F, though the optimal temperature is 70° to 80°F. (See "Time, Temperature, and Measurements" on page 54.) The gas forms bubbles that in turn expand in the oven to cause the bread to rise as it bakes. (Quick breads depend on chemical leaveners like baking powder or soda to generate gas; they're not fermented.)

The small amount of commercial yeast in that lump of dough we use to get our starter going is enough to get the natural fermentation process rolling. That bit of dough, plus more flour and water, then becomes an environment where other favorable yeasts and bacteria present in your kitchen and in the grain itself are nurtured. After a few days of feeding, those other organisms take hold, and the starter—now unique to your kitchen—is ready for baking.

To us this is wildly exciting, akin to growing your own vegetables or raising your own animals. (Some call raising a natural starter "microfarming.") It's more than thrilling: With repeated uses and feedings, the yeasts and bacteria develop and change, and the starter evolves.

And the acids and other by-products of this process add nuance and complexity to the starter, and in turn the baked goods. So your bread will not only be healthier than white bread leavened with commercial yeast, it'll be tastier.

Although the starter itself can be quite strong in flavor, it mellows when used to make dough. Our jumpstarter method—the pre-ferment mixture that is the foundation of most of these recipes—prevents the bread from becoming too sour, while providing a stable foundation for the dough to mature slowly. All of this, together, gives you rounded, nutty, mellow whole grain flavor.

ELASTICITY AND STRENGTH

And there's more. The energy produced by the starter gives natural fermentation the power to vastly improve the texture of whole grain bread.

Because whole grain flour retains bran and germ, it makes it more challenging for dough to rise. Remember that the endosperm contains the bulk of starch and the gluten-forming proteins—which give doughs elasticity and strength—so there's a higher concentration of this valuable component in white flour than in whole wheat. To further complicate the rising process, the sharp edges of bran can tear and hinder the development of the exact structure in the dough you're trying to build. In order to trap the gas created by fermentation, to develop dough that can stretch without tearing, you need the slow metabolism of natural starter.

Using a naturally fermented starter in the presence of lots of water, over a long period of time, allows whole wheat dough to develop the structure necessary to achieve a bread that's light, springy, chewy, and crisp crusted. Commercial yeast produces gas too quickly for this to happen. Plus, the starter itself is already elastic and strong, giving the dough a boost from the get-go.

When starter works its magic on whole grain doughs, you'll see visible webbing, and the dough will be stretchy, like taffy. The starch in the flour will puff to absorb water and help trap gas. You will notice all this happen as you go through the folds in the Bittman Bread recipe. The dough changes with each passing minute, and it's nothing short of miraculous.

WHOLE WHEAT FLOURS

We have baked these breads with scores of different flours, from mass-produced supermarket flours, to specialty regional and local flours, to flour we've ground ourselves (see the section that follows on page 36). The taste, texture, and overall experience varied greatly and unpredictably. While some of the surprises were fun, others were, well, annoying. We want consistency from our recipes.

You can get that if you bake our recipes with any commercially produced whole grain flour labeled "all-purpose" or "bread." (In general, whole wheat pastry flours won't develop enough strength and elasticity for bread, though they're fine for our torte, pancake, and beignet recipes.) You won't know the specific varieties of wheat contained in these flours, and they're almost always blends anyway, produced precisely so you will get consistency.

Many of these are very good, and the best (we've found) are the organic flours from Bob's Red Mill, King Arthur Baking Company, and Whole Foods. This is not to say only these will work—we've made spectacular breads with mass produced flour from companies like Pillsbury.

A WORD ABOUT GLUTEN

Any mention of gluten can freak people out. This makes sense for the roughly 1 percent of the population with celiac disease, and for those who react badly to gluten.

But gluten is essential to making traditional wheat breads (and to making anything you want to leaven, really), and studies have found that even people who are gluten sensitive can better tolerate naturally fermented whole grain breads. The thinking is that the slow fermentation process predigests the gluten so the body handles it more easily.

In addition, the presence of the fiber and germ slows down the way most people metabolize the grain's protein and starch, which can make eating whole wheat bread an option for those who are concerned about controlling their blood sugar or have similar metabolic or glucose issues. (If you have these health concerns, always check with your doctor first, of course.)

You can also get a variety of good flour online. As of this writing, our favorites are Community Grains (Mark loves their Patwin variety) and Cairnspring Mills (we both love their Expresso and have had great success with Yecora when we could get it), but our list grows as more good wheat is farmed around the country.

Wheat is grown in almost every state, and it's not impossible for you to find whole grain or flour that was raised nearby, even in a supermarket, though you're more likely to find it at a farmers' market (direct from the farm) or in a specialty store. These wheats are less predictable, more exciting, and often far more flavorful than anything we've mentioned above. If you're into experimenting and learning by doing, by all means try them. You'll be supporting small farmers and helping keep less-commercial strains of wheat viable.

Again, this kind of exploration is not for everyone. If you're satisfied with the results you get from Bob's Red Mill or King Arthur and you don't want to play around with different flavors and textures, then don't. Every time you change flour you will find subtle differences are needed in your technique, and your bread's vital characteristics will change, sometimes in ways you might not like.

Think of it like choosing wine. Some people have a house wine they buy for years and are happy with; some people never buy the same bottle twice, willing to take a chance on something new, even if they might not like it. Not all varieties of whole wheat flours are ideal for bread baking, and even if one batch is, the next year might bring changes to a given variety—wheat is a living thing, after all. But to us, the investigation is part of the fun. The Bittman Bread recipe includes a big section on how to "read" the dough (page 85) that will help you work with virtually any flour. Again, none of this is required. If you discover a flour you like and want to stick to it, that is a good way to go.

Many bakers are obsessed with protein content (usually described as a percentage, and in terms of strength higher is theoretically better), but we've found it's less important than the variety of wheat. With whole wheat, you're going to get a fair amount of protein anyway, usually more than 11 percent. Professionals also talk about the extraction rate, ash content, and the falling number. It would take us a long time to explain what these mean, and we don't want you to care. (Honestly—this is Mark speaking—I don't pay any attention to any of this. What's included here is more than enough to make excellent bread.)

There is another question worth considering: whether your preground flour is actually 100 percent whole grain. That's not easily answered since government regulations allow flours that have some of the bran and germ sifted out, which can increase their shelf life, to still be labeled "whole," even though technically they are not. This is a question you can expect to be answered honestly when you buy directly from a mill or an online distributor like those mentioned above. With supermarket flours, you can do some research online, or assume the best.

As with any food, if you buy from someone you trust, you have a good idea what you're getting. With flour, the other alternative is to start with a whole berry and grind it yourself. We're not exactly recommending that you do this—and we're certainly not insisting on it—but it's an option. Increasingly that's what Mark does, so we're going to switch to his voice for this next section.

GYOG (GRIND YOUR OWN GRAINS)

I never would've believed I'd buy a grain mill (remember, this is Mark talking now). But since almost every food is better when processed at the last minute, I thought I'd give it a shot and bought the cheapest mill that devotees seemed to agree was useful— the KoMo Mio. (I bought it from Pleasant Hill Grain, a friendly and helpful operation.)

It took some time to figure out what I was doing, but I am now hooked. In fact, given that you're unlikely to spend tens of thousands of dollars on an oven, and given that our process requires very little equipment overall, the biggest difference you can make in the quality of your bread— once you've mastered our techniques—is by using better, fresher flour. And the way to do that is to grind your own.

We can assume that fresh-ground flour is better from the perspective of nutrients: Grains themselves keep for at least a year if they're stored in a moderate and dry environment, but flours do not, because grinding exposes the inside of the kernels to oxygen. Although the nutritional advantages of preground whole grains over white flour remain overwhelming, freshly ground flour is even better. As with freshly ground coffee, fresh flour simply tastes better. (And in general, the finer you can grind your flour, the better.)

Having said all that, I've bought wheat that simply didn't taste that great, and some that didn't perform that well, no matter what adjustments I made. And that's frustrating. Furthermore, I've invested a lot of time figuring out just how to treat an especially temperamental batch of wheat to get the most out of it. That's satisfying in the end, but it's also a big time suck, and especially annoying when you then run out of that flour and have to move on.

However, I will also say that the best breads I've made are from flours I've milled myself—from Community Grains' Patwin wheat, from wheats I've sampled from the WSU Breadlab in Burlington, Washington, and from varieties distributed by GrowNYC's Grains project in New York City. So . . . this might be a route that interests you.

That's as far as I will bring you. I'm not going to start exploring the kinds of mills I might move on to, or the kinds of milling stones that might produce even better flour. I'm happy grinding my own wheat on the machine I've got. If any of this sounds appealing to you, go for it. And if it doesn't, buy the flour you like and stick with it. (That's what works for Kerri and millions of other people.)

Using Other Ingredients in These Recipes

Our basic bread has three ingredients: flour, water, and salt. (Starter is water and flour.)

Flour we've discussed. Water: If your tap water doesn't taste good, use distilled or spring water. Salt is optional, but unless you're making a traditional Tuscan unsalted bread or limit sodium for medical reasons, you should opt for it. Salt helps the dough two ways: A moderate amount will regulate yeast activity so fermentation is neither too fast nor too slow; and salt helps improve the strength of the wheat proteins as the dough develops. Commercial table salt (not iodized, please; it can taste metallic) is strong-tasting and hypersalty, but works fine. Kosher salt is a good alternative. Higher priced sea salts will bring more character; if your palate can tell the difference, and you want to go that route, feel free.

Beyond wheat lies a world of other grains. Rye is the second-most important bread flour, with incomparable flavor and an ability to add to a splendidly tough, crunchy crust. It's also tricky as hell. An experienced baker said to us a couple of years ago, "Whole grain baking is hard enough; why complicate it with rye?"

The answer is: Because rye tastes so damned good. The key to baking with rye is to either go all the way and make a Scandinavian-style bread—dense, sour, and incredibly delicious (Travel Bread, page 121)—or to use rye judiciously, at around 10 or at the most 20 percent of your total flour by weight. (In our basic recipe, that would mean 30 to 60 grams.) More than that and your dough will become difficult and unpredictable. (Try it, though; you'll learn a lot.) And note that when you buy rye flour, you'll sometimes see light and dark options; dark is whole grain, and what we prefer.

Almost any other flour can be used in those same proportions. Buckwheat brings beautiful color and distinctive flavor; barley helps create wonderful crusts; cornmeal adds crunch; rice, chickpea, fava, almond—all are interesting, different, wonderful. You might also try ancient wheats like einkorn, spelt, and farro, which can be used in higher proportions. All of this is part of the fun.

A word here about storing whole grains and flours: Since they include the germ and the bran, they're oilier than white flours, which means they spoil faster, especially in warm, humid weather. If you're baking weekly, you'll go through a five-pound bag in less than a month. If you bake more than that you might consider buying larger

quantities and storing them in airtight containers in a cool place. We've had no problems with off flavors following storage up to three months. If you want to keep flour longer than that, we recommend storing it in airtight containers in the fridge or freezer.

Cracked grains (usually soaked first) and seeds are other options. We call for caraway seeds in Mark's Rye (page 103), but almost all seeds—fennel, sunflower, cumin, poppy, sesame, pepitas, whatever—are used in traditional loaves around the world, and all add flavor and texture. Again, stay in the range of no more than 10 percent of the weight of the flour, at least until you get a feel for it. Ditto chopped nuts; we prefer skin-on raw or roasted unsalted almonds, walnuts, pecans, pistachios, and hazelnuts. Dried fruit is also good; see page 80. And ground spices (cinnamon, saffron, cardamom) or chopped fresh herbs (rosemary and lavender in particular) are welcome in small quantities.

A handful of recipes use dairy: milk or buttermilk instead of water in the jumpstarter; butter for melting or creaming with sugar for the cookies and torte; and cheese as a pizza topping, of course, but also baked into a couple of variations.

In keeping with the whole grain theme, we developed the sweet recipes with turbinado or minimally processed

("raw") sugar, as much for philosophical as flavor reasons, though the slight molasses, caramelly flavor works well with whole wheat. Granulated white sugar is fine too.

The Tools You'll Need

You don't need much to bake Bittman Bread or any of the other recipes in this book. But there are some essentials. Fortunately, you probably have most of them already. Here's the list:

Scale. Simply put, weighing is the best way to measure for baking with whole grains—and it doesn't take much getting used to. Weights more easily demonstrate the ratios between ingredients and help you make adjustments in ways volume just can't. Good-quality digital scales run less than $30 and last for years. If you want to bake with cups and spoons, try the conversions given in "Converting Weight to Volume" on page 43. But really, it's better to weigh. When you get the hang of it, you can eyeball, you can use volume, you can guess, and all of that will be fine. But for learning: Weigh. Please.

Container for starter. Your starter needs a place to live between uses. Glass is best, though we've both also used plastic. The container should be at least 1 quart in volume and have a tight-fitting lid. (Whether you tighten the lid or just let it rest over the container is up to you.) The starter will bubble and expand, so the most important thing is that the vessel is big enough to accommodate expansion.

Loaf pan. For sandwich breads, the recipes are calibrated for a standard loaf pan measuring 8½ x 4½ x 2¾ inches. Again: Don't use glass.

8- or 9-inch square or round baking pan or 9- or 10-inch ovenproof cast-iron or carbon-steel skillet. The Focaccia, some of the variations of Garlicky Dinner Rolls, the Cinnamon Rolls, and Chocolate Chunk Torte all work in any of these pans. The torte is fine baked in glass but the others are best in metal.

Pizza pans and baking stones. Mark has a baking stone in his oven and uses that for everything—he just sets whatever pot or pan right on the stone, then uses the stone instead of the oven rack for the final bake on the breads. Kerri only drags out the stone for pizzas. If you're going to make pizza a lot, you'll want a stone for sure, and probably a couple of round pizza pans; see the Pizza recipe on page 139 for specific pan options.

Other pans. Large rimmed baking sheets, cookie sheets, a muffin tin with standard-size cups—all handy if you want to bake baguettes, biscuits, rolls, and cookies. For the beignets in this book you'll need a deep fryer or a heavy pot big enough to hold a couple of inches of oil with several inches of space above it.

Parchment paper, brown or white. You can't bake much in this book without it. And neither lining pans in wax paper nor foil will work. (You can buy packages of sheets instead of rolls, and they're very handy.) Some of the very thin sheets may burn or stick on the bottom of the loaf a little. If that happens to you, try moving the oven rack up one notch higher or try another brand of parchment. We've had good luck with the unbleached so-called natural parchment. Whatever you use, expect the overhang outside the pot to singe and darken; if that concerns you—it needn't—just cut it closer to the lid.

Bowls, spoons, and other tools. Besides a 1-quart jar to house your starter, you'll need a couple of bowls. Many of the how-to shots in the book show a broad-bottomed bowl like the one Kerri uses, in which she can fold the dough. Mark works in a smaller, deeper bowl and folds on a wet

---

"THE POT"

We usually bake Bittman Bread and the other boule-style round loaves in a (roughly) 2-quart Dutch oven with a lid (we favor the one made by Lodge); cast-iron is ideal, but as long as your vessel is ovenproof to 500°F, you're fine.

Our standard pot is smaller than most heavy braising pots, but we like this size for ease of handling, and for a two-person household that will presumably take a couple of days, or even longer, to work through it.

If you eat more bread, or have more people, there are many options: Use a 4½- or 5-quart ovenproof pot (the most common size) and either make the Big Bittman Bread variation; or use anything in between, and scale the recipe accordingly. If you want to make a standard loaf but only have a big pot, fit the bottom of the pot with a ring of crumpled foil, leaving a 6- to 7-inch open space, creating a kind of pot in a pot; line that with parchment. A 2- to 3-quart ovenproof saucepan with a fitted lid also works, even if it's got a single handle; you can increase the recipe by 25 percent to fill a 3-quart pan nicely.

Everything works: we've used cast iron—enameled and uncoated—ceramic, and stainless and carbonized steel from several manufacturers, in all sizes. Just no glass, please, and of course nothing with plastic or wood handles.

---

surface. Either way is fine. A big silicone or rubber spatula or large spoon is handy for mixing doughs, as is a pastry blade (aka bench scraper) for moving dough easily. An electric mixer is handy for the cake, and you'll need a food processor for the cookies.

Lame, razor blade, or sharp kitchen scissors. Pronounced *lahm*, a lame is the French word for a razor blade tool used to slash the top of loaves before baking. Mark prefers a naked razor blade, which is just as good. You can also use sharp scissors (as Kerri usually does), but we've found the doughs are generally too wet for even the sharpest knives to make a good cut. (There's more detail about slashing starting on page 72.)

Knife and cutting board (or slicing machine). Mark uses a semiprofessional rotary deli slicer for cutting even slices of bread, which can be made very, very thin.

Kerri doesn't really have room (that kitchen you see in the photographs was a loaner!) so she goes old school with a knife and a big, heavy wooden cutting board. Be sure the blade is serrated and at least 10 inches long, especially if you like your slices thin.

Instant-read thermometer. Doesn't have to be fancy. But until you get the hang of how the different breads bake in your oven, you won't know for sure if the loaf is ready unless you check the interior temperature.

Mills. Mark really likes his KoMo Mio, but he readily confesses to not being an expert in this department. If you want to go the home-grinding route, be sure you have a good source of wheat berries and do a little research: Some mills are electric; others are hand-crank. The milling surfaces vary a lot, and the price range is huge. As Mark said on page 36, the folks at Pleasant Hill Grain are friendly and helpful.

CONVERTING WEIGHT TO VOLUME

The ingredient amounts in all the recipes except Beginner Bittman Bread are expressed in grams. We explain why in the "Scale" entry on page 40. But if you want to try baking without a scale, knowing that we strongly recommend you weigh ingredients, this will help you succeed in measuring by volume.

We considered including a conversion chart, but all flours are of different density—that is, a given volume will not give consistent weight. (Having said that, Bob's Red Mill, King Arthur Baking Company, and other reliable sources have conversion charts on their websites.)

In general, it's best to lowball the water, especially at the beginning. So to make jumpstarter you'd use ¾ cup starter, about 6 tablespoons water, and ½ cup flour. For the dough you'd add 1½ cups flour and ¾ cup water.

Then adjust as necessary. As long as proportions are close—twice as much flour by volume as water—you can make any size loaf, provided of course you err on the side of not-too-much with the water at the beginning. You can add water, but you can't take it out. (Well, you could add flour to compensate, but that's much trickier.)

You can measure volume with handfuls or coffee cups—just be mindful that our basic recipe fits the 2-quart pot perfectly, and if you go bigger, you'll need to find the right pot for your bigger loaves.

So here are some guidelines, though what we really hope is that they'll convince you that weighing is easier:

- **100 grams whole wheat flour is about ¾ cup.**

- **100 grams water is about 6 tablespoons (in any case, a smidge less than half the volume of flour)**

- **100 grams whole wheat starter straight out of the fridge will be about ½ cup. If it's on the wet, pourable side, it might be more; if it is warm and active it will puff up more.**

- **Figure 7 grams salt to be 1 slightly heaping teaspoon.**

Ban the Banneton

KC:

Our readers are probably wondering why we don't use a proofing basket— the banneton that crossed over from professional bakers to home enthusiasts during the recent sourdough craze. Let's tell the story about why we stopped proofing dough in the banneton, added parchment, and went with a cold-pot method.

MB:

It's all related and all key. Though that heated-pot technique in the original no-knead recipe was the last part of the process we abandoned. You deserve the credit for this, so you start.

KC:

From the beginning I had more trouble with the banneton than you did. Whenever I turned my dough upside down to transfer it to the hot pot, it deflated. Maybe the basket wasn't seasoned with enough flour, or I just plain got panicky, but there was almost always a hitch. And of course the loaf would be never quite dome right after that trauma.

MB:

I'm sure that's a common problem. My dough sometimes deflated in transferring too, and I've had that discussion with lots of people. I remember you started looking for alternatives. I tried so many fixes I can't count them. But because the dough is wet and soft, it was just a huge challenge.

KC:

Since you and Jim Lahey first put no-knead pot-baked bread into the mainstream, people have offered all sorts of spins and potential improvements. We spent at least a couple of months swapping out different variables one at a time, each new twist punctuated with exclamation points and excited profanities in our notes. One day all the techniques and methods we tried sorted themselves out in my head, and I woke up thinking we should try a cold parchment paper–lined pot—and finally ban the banneton for good. And then you said . . .

MB:

Why do we even need to turn the dough upside down? I bet after the last fold we can just tuck the edges underneath, shape it into a ball, and plop it into the cold, parchment-lined pot; then do that final fermentation right in the pot, just long enough to let the dough recover after folding and moving.

KC:

Presto. Now getting the dough into the pot is easy and foolproof, especially with whole grain doughs. And we've expanded the principle to many of the other recipes in the book. The difference in ease is phenomenal.

Glossary

We work hard to avoid jargon, to speak and write simply. Nevertheless, there are some words specific to bread making that you may want to at least know in case you get bitten by the bug and start digging around, doing your own research.

Acidity. Acid is a by-product of fermentation, so all naturally fermented starters are "sour." But with whole grain dough that acidity is balanced by the slight sweet and bitter tastes of the bran and germ. Using an established starter and our jumpstarter technique also helps mellow the flavors. This is why we try to avoid referring to the starter or bread as "sourdough"—it's acidic enough to have flavor, but in general, naturally fermented dough shouldn't have so much acid that it tastes sour. Ours does not.

Autolyse. A technical term that simply refers to the period when the dough rests after mixing, but before salt is added. The purpose is to give the freshly watered and agitated wheat proteins and starches a chance to regroup and form the webbing that will eventually make the dough elastic and strong. This is what we mean in the recipes when we say "let it sit" for an hour after mixing the dough and before adding salt and beginning the folds.

Crumb. The inside of bread or any other baked food like cake or cookies. You will be surprised at how much it varies. A good crumb in Bittman Bread has lots of holes (see below; some may even be pretty big) and is moist and chewy.

Crust. The outside. In Bittman Bread, we like this tough and with a bit of crunch.

Elasticity and strength. Professional bakers would say "elasticity and extensibility." These terms seem less confusing. Elasticity is the stretchiness of the dough; strength is how well it forms a web that encloses the expanding gas bubbles produced by fermentation. There's more on how dough develops these characteristics on page 34.

Feeding. Adding flour and water to starter, after removing some for use or if it has been ignored for a week or so. The yeast in starter needs to be fed to stay alive and active.

Fermentation. The natural metabolic process that converts sugars and starches into acid and gas. The gas forms bubbles that in turn expand in the oven to cause bread to rise as it bakes.

Holes. During baking, air bubbles leave holes in the crumb (and sometimes the crust); they keep bread light. When holes get too big and firm they're called "tunnels" (see below).

Hydration. The amount of water in the dough, expressed as a percentage of the flour. So if you have a dough that's 100 grams flour and 100 grams water, that's 100% hydration. (It's almost as loose as a batter, more like starter.)

Jumpstarter. Our name for the basic pre-ferment technique we use; see "Pre-ferment" below.

Lame. A slashing tool, like a curved razor blade in a handle. Used to cut into the top of the dough so it expands evenly.

Pre-ferment. As the word implies, this is a mixture that ferments *before* the whole dough. What we call "jumpstarter" is a less-than-classic pre-ferment. The technical names for classic pre-ferments are *old dough, sponge, poolish* (French), and *biga* (Italian).

Proofing (and over-proofing). Technically, the final fermentation of dough, after it has been shaped. But it can also refer to proofing yeast—that is, mixing yeast with water and letting it start to grow. So to avoid confusion we use the words *ferment, fermentation, mature, puff,* and *rise* instead. We still use *overproofing* to describe the dough when it ferments long enough that it starts to puff and bubble with too much gas, which can cause the bread to collapse in places during baking.

Sourdough. Not our favorite descriptor. See "Acidity" above.

Starch. Another word for a carbohydrate, like those found in the endosperm of grains. When you metabolize or refine starch—in the human body, during fermentation, or while processing food—you get sugar. In the case of wheat kernels, the protein and fat in the germ and the bran slow the conversion of starch into sugar so the grain is more digestible and nutritious.

Starter. A mixture of water and flour for cultivating yeasts and favorable bacteria (via a fermentation process) to use for leavening doughs.

Tunnel. A big hole, usually defined by a firm ring of dough, that can bore an inch or more into the crumb. Tunneling is variously believed to be caused by too much or too little water, low-protein flour, or incomplete folding as the dough develops, and can happen to even the best bakers. We try not to freak out about it. If you're getting a lot of tunnels, or really big ones, start troubleshooting by reviewing "Reading the Dough" on page 84. Be sure to gently bring the dough back together after the folds and give it enough time to recover and rise again before proceeding.

Yeast. A single-cell fungus that converts carbohydrates (sugars and starches) into alcohol and carbon dioxide. In other words, the stuff you need to make doughs bubble and breads rise during baking. You can buy it in packages or jars (or less often, in cakes) or cultivate your own in a naturally fermented starter.

CHAPTER 3

BITTMAN BREAD

The loaf to rule them all

Big Bittman Bread, page 82

W E'VE COLLABORATED ON THOUSANDS of recipes over the years, and none has been remotely like this one. It's the culmination of our quest to codify and share our experiences with what we have come to believe is the easiest, most flexible, and forgiving way to make the best breads ever.

Our bread is unlike any 100 percent whole wheat bread you've eaten. And we're confident once you dive into this chapter and bake your first loaf, you'll be hooked.

What follows in this core chapter is a detailed, elaborate scenario that walks you through every step of producing a fine, uncomplicated, absolutely delicious whole grain bread. And in this process you will find peace, love, enjoyment, and fulfillment—seriously—as well as a link to the history of hundreds of millions of bread makers.

Though the work itself is almost ludicrously simple and uses precisely three ingredients (two of which are salt and water!), the process, which recruits dozens of strains of yeasts and millions of individual organisms, is complex and never completely under your control. The flour—even of the same brand, whether store-bought or home-ground—changes from bag to bag. Temperature changes from day to day. Yeasts evolve, and no matter how consistently you treat it, your starter will be moody, a living thing that in turn must fuel another living thing, the dough.

Perfection—or, really, near-perfection—is a moving target, but once you start to get close, your bread will be better and more consistent. It'll still change, but you'll settle into a pattern that will always give you spectacular bread. Until then, the rare true failure will teach you something you'll be glad to know.

We've made many mistakes, and you will too, especially if you play with different grains and flours. We've seen dough overinflate and deflate; tunnels big enough to put your pinky through; tight, dense crumb; breads that barely rose at all.

We offer many ways to understand creating the essential loaf: troubleshooting, variations, and the benefit of years of experience and exploring. On the pages that follow, the left side offers barebones guidance, designed so you can quickly refer back to it whenever you need to; the right side more detail and nuance.

What to Expect in This Chapter

Once you have starter (page 16), the process is made up of five steps, beginning with a "jumpstarter," an innovative spin on what professionals call a "pre-ferment" (that is, a bit of dough that is fermented in advance), an important part of natural bread making. (We're keeping jargon to a minimum, but see the Glossary on page 46 for more details.) This sits overnight, or for 8 to 12 hours whenever that's convenient for you. You can make jumpstarter in the morning and bread at night, or jumpstarter at night and bread in the morning, or any other pace you like. You can also, as you'll see, use the fridge at any point to slow down the process. So you can make jumpstarter in the morning, refrigerate it, and pick it up again the next morning. With the refrigerator, the variations of the pace are pretty much infinite; see "Baking Bread on Any Schedule" on page 89.

Starter is temperamental; the jumpstarter evens out the many variables and promotes consistency. By mixing a predetermined amount of starter with fresh flour and water, in the same way every time, you end up with a mixture that supplies roughly the same amount of energy to cause your dough to rise. That in turn will develop the strength and elasticity the dough requires to yield beautifully risen bread with a pleasant interior and fantastic crust. The jumpstarter also helps the bread develop a wheaty, complex, slightly acidic flavor that's not overly sour.

When the jumpstarter is ready, you build the dough and let it sit for an hour or so. During this time, the proteins in the flour continue to develop. The third stage is equally easy: You season the dough with salt and add a little more water. This is also the time for any other additions you might like.

Next come the folds, where dramatic changes take place over a period of a couple of hours. The folds are just what they sound like—you press out the dough and fold it over itself, using water (not flour) to keep your hands from sticking. Then you transfer the dough to a parchment paper–lined pot, rest it a bit, then put the covered pot in a cold oven. And finally, you bake. This process essentially creates a combination proofing box and hearth oven. As the lid traps heat, the loaf generates steam, inflating and stretching the dough before the crust becomes too hard for it to expand. Once the lid comes off about halfway through baking, the crust starts to form and develop into a crisp, golden-brown exterior while the dough (now bread, really) finishes "naked" in the oven.

The pages surrounding the recipe are full of visual and verbal backroads dotted with technical details. Our hope is to provide at-a-glance information in a format that's both linear and compartmentalized, without being complicated.

It is an easy process but a mindful one; if you're not paying attention, things may not go well. It's also not without risks. There may be what seem like failures, especially at the beginning. But the rewards are indescribable, a reintroduction to the staff of life and a way of interacting with nature that will improve your well-being. And your eating.

TIME, TEMPERATURE, AND MEASUREMENTS

Just about everything involved in baking Bittman Bread is flexible and not fussy. There are a range of times and temperatures that will work well for making the jumpstarter and maturing (that is, fermenting) dough. (To learn what's going on during that process, see the Glossary on page 46.) As long as your ambient room temperature is between 65° and 80°F, the timing here and in the other recipes will work; the dough will develop just fine at higher and lower temperatures, too (within reason), but at the extreme ends the process will speed up or slow down noticeably. (When Mark baked in a kitchen that was over 80°F, his jumpstarter was bubbling and puffed after just 6 hours.)

There are subtle flavor differences, too, between dough that ferments slowly versus one that rises at a sprint, but those differences are not as pronounced as the ones that come about from, for example, changing flours or flour combinations.

Measuring is similarly variable, even though the recipes list specific weights as starting points. We make the case for using a scale instead of cups and spoons on page 40. Once you get acquainted with thinking in grams, it's easier to adjust in small increments—and simply forgive minor imprecisions—as you gain more experience and depend on visual cues.

After a few loaves, instead of strictly following the recipe, you'll become confident, adding a few more or fewer grams water or flour here and there to the starter (page 16), the jumpstarter (page 57), and/or the dough (page 60). As a general rule, you want to give this dough as much water as it will take, but when the exterior of the dough becomes milky, or there's a puddle in the bottom of your bowl or on the work surface . . . that's too much. You will learn how to stop before then, but meanwhile measuring and working in small steps are important.

Bittman Bread

Time

18 to 24 hours, with intermittent activity and lots of flexibility

one: **Jumpstarter**

100 grams whole wheat starter (see the directions on page 16)

100 grams water, plus 50 grams for feeding the starter

100 grams whole wheat flour, plus 50 grams for feeding the starter

1

Combine the starter, 100 grams water, and 100 grams flour in a large bowl. Stir with a rubber spatula or large spoon until the jumpstarter comes together in a loose dough or a thick batter, with no traces of dry flour remaining. Cover the bowl with plastic or a damp kitchen towel.

2

Feed the starter: Add 50 grams each water and whole wheat flour to the starter remaining in the container and stir or shake until well mixed. Cover and return it to the refrigerator.

● If you use a broad, flat-bottomed bowl, you can execute the whole process, including folding, right in there. A deeper, narrower bowl means that you'll have to do your folds on a cutting board or clean work surface. Either is fine; see the photos on pages 65–67.

❶ The seal need not be airtight; you just want to prevent the jumpstarter (and later the dough) from drying out on top.

❷ Feeding the starter when you make the jumpstarter is a good habit. You take the container from the fridge, use what the recipe directs, then replace that weight in flour and water, stir well, re-cover, and refrigerate the container until the next time you bake.

For more detail about how, when, and what to feed the starter—and how to explore other flours, ratios, and schedules—see page 90.

(opposite) The jumpstarter changes dramatically as it ferments: As the starter feeds on the additional water and flour. You can use it any time within the 8-to-12-hour window when the bubbling and spreading are at their peak.

continued →

3

Let the jumpstarter sit at room temperature for at least 8 or up to 12 hours before proceeding. The jumpstarter will thin, spread, or rise (depending on your bowl) and become active, with live and popped bubbles. (See the photos on pages 56 and 59.)

❸ If you want to bake in the morning, start the jumpstarter at night; if you want to bake in the afternoon or evening, start it in the morning. Anything in the 8-to-12-hour range works, but if your room is warm, you probably want to move on more quickly than if it's cool. (At 80°F, a 12-hour rise is too long; at 65°F, 8 hours is too short.) You'll quickly learn to see when the jumpstarter is ready, and it's not a single moment. To bake during the day, we usually start jumpstarter sometime before bed and pick it up sometime after a morning coffee. You can adjust the timing during any stage of this process to fit your schedule; see page 89.

(oppposite) **Watch the bubbles:** After the jumpstarter has sat for about 12 hours, however, it starts to lose power. The bubbles become smaller and most of them will have popped; try not to let yours get to this stage. If you need to delay making the dough or if you see the jumpstarter starting to wane, refrigerate it. This will slow the action for up to 24 hours. You can also refrigerate the dough into hibernation at any stage in the process; see page 89 for all the options.

two: **Dough**

200 grams whole wheat flour

110 grams water, plus more if needed

1
Add the flour and water to the jumpstarter. Again, mix with a rubber spatula or big spoon. The dough should be shaggy and sticky, but not runny like batter. If you can't incorporate all the flour, add more water 5 grams (1 teaspoon, or a little dribble) at a time as you stir.

2
Cover the bowl the same way you did the jumpstarter and let the dough sit for about an hour.

● This step includes resting time that professional bakers call "autolyse." It's an important pause that allows the dough to relax before salt is added so the fiber and protein components of the flour can reorganize and build the foundation for the elasticity and strength necessary to get a light and open interior crumb.

❶ How much water you add to make the dough can vary, even with the same flour. Heat, humidity, the maturity of your starter, and the amount of water in the starter will all effect how much the flour absorbs.

At first you may be uncomfortable with a wetter dough, but it's actually easy, and you'll get used to it. A relatively high concentration of water (nearly as much, by weight, as flour) helps the dough develop strength and generate steam during baking, which in turn leads to better rise, flavor, and texture.

Over the entire process your dough might absorb up to 75 grams more water (a little less than ⅓ cup) during the folds. It's not impossible to get to an extra 90 grams (a scant ½ cup), which would make your dough equal parts water and flour or 100% hydrated. See "Is Wetter Better?" on page 96.

❷ You can cut this rest to 45 minutes, but a full hour or even a little longer is best.

Mix: Adding flour and water to the jumpstarter until it forms a uniform but shaggy dough will require the most vigorous mixing and handling in the entire process.

Rest: Letting the dough rest after mixing and before adding salt gives the proteins in the flour a chance to relax, regroup, and begin to form the webbing that ultimately gives the dough strength and elasticity. (This is the step technically known as "autolyse.")

Add: Sprinkle the salt over the top of the dough and wet your hands generously before folding it in.

Mix gently: Use your fingertips to lightly dimple the dough to distribute the salt, adding a few more drops of water if it gets sticky or gritty. Then fold once or twice and tuck the edges under into a ball. The dough will feel stiffer and be far less shaggy than before.

three: Season

7 grams salt

1

Sprinkle the salt over the dough. Wet your hands and incorporate the salt by turning and folding the dough over itself in the bowl or on the work surface. Keep turning the dough and wetting your hands, the dough, and the bowl or surface if necessary to prevent sticking. Fold and turn the dough until it is no longer lumpy but relatively smooth. Pressing lightly with your fingertips to make dimples helps incorporate additions quickly, but you'll find a style that feels right to you. (See the photos at left.)

2

If you're going to add seeds, nuts, dried fruit, cracked or soaked grains, whatever, sprinkle them in with the salt.

3

If you were working on a surface, put the dough back in the bowl and cover it. Let the dough sit again anywhere from 15 to 30 minutes, depending on the temperature of the room and how lively the dough is: It should puff slightly and have some spring and movement when you touch it; you'll notice the difference.

● A gram of salt more or less than what we recommend is a matter of taste, and the differences are subtle, with virtually no impact on the finished bread. If you omit the salt entirely, though, the dough won't develop the strength to rise properly and the bread will taste a little strange to most people. See page 37.

❶ You'll always use water, *not flour*, to handle this dough. Mark works by the sink so he can repeatedly run his hands under the faucet and splash water onto the cutting board. Kerri keeps a bowl of water on the counter, dipping her hands and/or splashing a little onto the dough. Figure about 25 grams water (5 teaspoons) for incorporating the salt.

❷ For ideas on additions, see the variations that follow (page 78) and the list on page 82. Keep the extras to no more than 100 grams total or the dough won't rise or bake properly. Always add just enough water to round and smooth the dough and press out lumps. If the dough starts to separate, or pieces fling themselves off, withhold water and keep working the dough in your hands until it holds itself together.

❸ The timing is less important than observing how the dough looks and feels. See page 85.

four: **Fold**

Four times while the dough ferments—every 30 minutes or so—you're going to handle it using a technique called a "fold," i.e. folding the dough. There are a couple ways to do this; see the directions in this section and the photos starting on the opposite page.

1
Lightly wet your hands and a large cutting board or clean work surface. Gently turn out the dough and press it out into a rough rectangle. Then fold it over on itself in thirds, letter style. If anything sticks, use a little more water. Within each "fold" you will repeat this action once or twice more, going the other direction.

OR

If the bottom of your bowl is wide and flat enough so that the dough is no more than 2 inches thick, you can work right in the bowl. Wet your hands and sprinkle a few drops on the dough. Press the dough into the bowl, dimpling it a bit with your fingers. Grab the dough on one end and hold it up, letting gravity stretch it. Just as it seems about to tear, fold it over the dough in the bowl, then stretch the other side and fold it on top. Repeat once or twice more, from another direction.

continued on page 70→

● Now you will incorporate small amounts of water as you fold the dough four times at 30-minute intervals, gradually giving the dough all the water it can handle but no more than that. This technique develops the starch and proteins in the flour, which form an elastic webbing to trap the gas given off during fermentation and baking. (Think of dough as a balloon of flour and water that fills with gas as it ferments and bakes.) A strong structure is what allows the dough to rise and the bread to become light and airy, forming open pockets in the interior.

❶ The importance of wetting your hands—and often the dough— during folding cannot be overstated: It prevents sticking for sure, while changing the dough before your eyes. As the dough ferments, the texture will become increasingly springy, webby, and elastic, and the exterior of the dough will develop a sheen. The trick is to achieve that without becoming too milky or shaggy, and losing the exact structure you're trying to build.

FOLDING THE DOUGH
KERRI'S WAY

(clockwise, from top left)
Kerri does all the folds right in her mixing bowl
since it's broad enough at the bottom to stretch
and press the dough about 1 inch thick. If this
works for you, start by grabbing one edge and pull
it until it almost breaks.

Like Mark, Kerri then folds the opposite sides
of the dough over into thirds and repeats once,
sometimes twice, if the dough feels too dry or stiff.
As the dough becomes more elastic and strong
she can actually pick up one edge, hold the rest
over the bowl, and with a little wiggling let gravity
stretch the dough before folding into thirds.

For the second part of the fold, Kerri stretches
the short edges of the dough over into thirds
before tucking and gathering into a ball the way
Mark does.

FOLDING THE DOUGH MARK'S WAY

(top) Mark starts by wetting his work surface and hands before transferring the dough from the bowl. Use outstretched fingers to flatten it by pressing purposefully but not too aggressively. You'll notice a slight milkiness to the water on the surface; that signals the dough doesn't need any more water than what it takes to keep your hands from sticking.

(center) Mark begins each of the four folds with an oval-ish shape, about ½ inch thick. It doesn't matter if the shape is irregular.

(bottom) Then he lightly stretches and folds the dough over itself in thirds: first from the edge of one long side, then from the other long edge so it looks like you folded a letter.

(top) Working from the short ends, next Mark folds the dough in thirds again from the other direction.

(center) And you're left with a multi-layered square. Again, press gently with flat fingers to help the dough come back together. (Here he's showing the first fold, so notice that the dough is rather shaggy; it will get smoother with each successive fold.)

(bottom) Mark finishes the fold by gathering the edges and corners of the square underneath the dough, tucking and rolling with his fingers and palms to seal a seam at the bottom and shape a ball.

DOUGH TEXTURE
AFTER EACH FOLD

(top) After the first fold: At the beginning the dough is rough and shaggy and not yet elastic enough to stretch much. You might need to incorporate some water at this stage—enough on your hands to create a sheen on the surface without causing a milky residue that doesn't fully absorb.

(bottom) After the second fold: The dough will be less rough and shaggy and begin to puff and get stretchy. You might even start to see some air bubbles. It might still absorb some water at this stage but be careful not to over-wet it.

(top) After the third fold: When you shape it into a ball it holds together better and is much smoother on the surface. Notice there's some sheen but not much of a milky residue on the work surface. And there should be more bubbles.

(bottom) After the fourth fold: When you did the folding this time, did the dough look so lively it seemed to be breathing as you handled it? The surface will be smooth and bubbles should be visible. Now it's ready for the pot.

2

Whichever method you use, wet your hands whenever necessary to prevent sticking. After repeating the motions a couple of times, gently fold or gather the edges, and press the dough back together with the tips of your fingers. Tuck under the edges underneath to form a loose ball, return it to the bowl (if it's not already there), cover, and let it rest at room temperature.

3

Repeat the folds about every 30 minutes, three more times for a total of four folds within about 2 hours. You'll probably add less water each time as the dough becomes more springy and stretchy.

❷ The dough will tell you when it can't absorb any more water: Watch for the slightly milky liquid to start forming; it will coat the bowl or cutting board, and maybe a little will sit on top of or around the edges of the dough. That's when to stop. Using more than enough to prevent sticking from this point on may cause the dough to become shaggy again and fall apart; you don't want that to happen. (For more details, see the photos on pages 68–69 and "Reading the Dough" on page 84.)

❸ A half-hour between folds is really a suggestion. You can rush a bit and cut it to 15 or 20 minutes. (Even 25 minutes, over four folds, gives you a little extra free time.) Or you might get distracted and let it go 45 minutes in between. Once you can read the dough, you can make adjustments on the fly. It's really hard to go far wrong here, as you'll see, and on page 89 you'll learn how to intentionally slow the process so you can be even more relaxed about time.

The transformation of the dough during folding is dramatic. For the first fold, you're working with a mostly unresponsive blob that is not yet completely smooth, still a little lumpy.

4

Sometime during the course of the folds, line your pot with a sheet of parchment paper, pressing it into the bottom and creasing it over the lip to keep it in place. There's a photo of this in the Beginner Bread recipe on page 20 and another on page 74.

When you press down on it, it spreads, a lot—it'll flatten to four or five times its size. But by the second fold, the dough is more elastic and smooth, and bounces back while you work it. It will still spread when you press it, but there's resistance.

The third fold finds the dough airy, light, smooth, elastic, resilient, and responsive—very much alive. At this point it's best to fold a little more gently; you're walking the line between developing gluten (which requires handling) and preserving those lovely air pockets (which requires delicacy).

The fourth fold is barely a fold; mostly you're rolling and tucking the dough round and round and round until it forms a ball. Just apply enough pressure to join any seams without deflating the air bubbles in the dough too much. (See the photo series on pages 68–69.) Those seams will always remain on the bottom.

4 Parchment paper is a must here; there is no substitute. Buying it in sheets rather than on a roll simplifies matters.

five: Bake

1

After the fourth fold, with just enough water on your hands to keep it from sticking, lift the ball, cupping your fingers under the bottom, and lower it into the center of the parchment paper–lined pot. Cover the pot with its lid and let it rest for 15 to 30 minutes.

2

Sprinkle the top of the dough with flour or seeds or salt—or don't. Make ¼- to ½-inch deep slashes on the top of the dough in an *X* pattern, a square, or three parallel lines.

3

Make sure the rack is in the middle of the oven. Put the covered pot on the rack and set the oven to 485°F. (Yes, you are starting with a cold oven.) Set a timer for 30 minutes.

continued→

● By starting with a covered pot in a cold oven, the dough produces gorgeous doming, a crisp crust, and a moist interior, what we consider an ideal bread. And the baking is fast and easy.

❶ Here you want to under- rather than overestimate time for the rest: Usually 15 minutes is plenty, and 20 almost always is. (The dough can even go straight to the oven with minimal impact on the rise and crumb.) You're just looking for the dough to recover from being moved. There should be some puffing, not too much (known as overproofing), which can cause the bread to collapse. The best test is to press a wet finger into the dough. If it holds the indent for a few seconds without springing back quickly, it's ready for the oven. If it is unresponsive, it has risen too much. You should bake the loaf anyway; usually overproofed bread is still enjoyable—and it's a learning experience.

❷ The dusting is just window dressing but always looks nice. Before slashing, put some flour in a fine-meshed strainer or powdered sugar shaker and scatter as much or as little as you like over the top of the dough.

The slashing helps make doming more uniform; if you don't do it, the dough will probably crack randomly

BAKING TIMES CAN BE VARIED, TOO

Everything about this process is flexible, and that includes baking times (and, when you gain experience, even temperatures).

The covered pot in a cold oven is absolutely the way to start, and there's no reason to change that or even think about it. But from then on the timing is variable: You can remove the lid after a half hour, but five or even ten minutes in either direction there won't matter much.

You can change procedure if you like by removing the lid and immediately taking the loaf out of the pot, lowering the temperature, and baking a bit longer. Mark likes to follow the overall recommended pattern—lid on, lid off, bread out—and then leave the loaf in the oven after it's turned off, even as long as a half-hour, to develop a darker crust. And we both forget to set timers sometimes. You will, too, and that will lead to discoveries that will determine your personal style.

You've got to be careful about burning, especially once you're baking at 485°F, but other than that, you have a lot of leeway. Doneness is really determined by color, hardness of crust, and internal temperature; given that, feel free to play.

somewhere. (It might do that even with slashing, but it's less likely.) That's not so terrible—it doesn't affect quality, just the bread's appearance and the shape of slices—but most people prefer an orderly look. Slash with an ordinary razor blade (best, we think), a French baking tool called a *lame* (pronounced *lahm,* essentially a curved razor blade in a handle), or sharp kitchen scissors. You want to go deep enough so the opening doesn't reseal, usually at least ¼ inch, depending on how springy your dough is. With experience, you might want to design your own slashing patterns for decoration.

❸ Every oven is different, but around 485°F is the optimal target. Use an oven thermometer to see how your oven behaves.

As the oven heats up in 15 minutes or so, the dough will experience a final burst of fermentation. As the heat rises, the water in the dough generates steam, keeping the crust moist enough to expand before it hardens from the high heat.

It's fine to have a pizza stone on the rack and put the pot on that. (Mark does; Kerri doesn't.) When you take the loaf out of the pot and place it directly on the stone to finish, the stone helps crisp and brown the bottom crust.

(top) Line the pot: Sometime before the fourth fold, cut a sheet of parchment big enough for it to drape over the edges after tucking it in. We don't fuss much with smoothing out the paper perfectly, but you do want to press it around the bottom edge to make sure you have good coverage.

(bottom) Cut the dough: Just before baking, slash the top with a razor blade that's either straight or curved (known as a *lame*) or snip with sharp kitchen scissors. The idea is to control where the loaf splits as it expands during baking. The design isn't important, but the cuts should be about ¼-inch deep.

74

(top) Bake in the pot: No matter how many loaves we make, the moment we remove the lid is always exciting. The change is so dramatic. Yours might not be this dark and that's fine. Everyone's oven behaves a little differently. Let the bread continue to bake uncovered until it darkens and smells like toast, another 10 to 15 minutes.

(bottom) Bake on the rack: Then lower the heat to 400°F, remove the pot from the oven, use the paper to lift out the bread and let it finish baking directly on the rack; or if you used a pizza stone put it right on that. The crust will brown evenly all over and it's done when the internal temperature is between 205°F and 210°F.

4

When the timer goes off, carefully remove the lid. Ideally the bread will have domed and the slashes opened a bit; you will see a pale crust. Now set the timer for 10 minutes. You want the crust to dry and harden enough to lift the loaf from the pot. If it's not quite ready, check again in 5 minutes.

5

Take the pot out of the oven and turn the heat down to 400°F. Remove the loaf from the pot and peel off the parchment.

6

Put the loaf back in the oven directly on the rack or on the pizza stone. Bake until the crust is dark and an instant-read thermometer inserted into the center of the loaf registers between 205° and 210°F, 15 to 30 minutes.

7

Transfer the bread to a wire rack. Cool completely before slicing.

4 Everyone's oven and pot behaves a little differently: If your oven takes longer than 15 minutes to come to 485°F, let the bread go 35 to 40 minutes before removing the lid.

5 Mark uses mitts for this; Kerri lifts the loaf out of the pot and onto the oven rack using the corners of the parchment paper, then shoves the bread off with a spatula.

6 Until you get used to your oven and how quickly it cools, keep a close eye on the bread at this stage. At the beginning, the temperature will still be quite high; you can hasten the cooling by leaving the oven door open a bit. In any case, the bread is almost always done when it reaches a color you like, and it's difficult to overbake it in this time frame.

7 The bread is hot, and even though warm bread sounds appealing, cutting it now will result in mushy, torn dough. Let it cool so the interior can set.

8

Rather than wrestle with the whole loaf, some people find it easier to halve the bread, put the cut side down, and slice downward through the crust.

9

The bread keeps for days, either face down on the counter (or a plate, board, or virtually any other hard surface) or wrapped in a clean kitchen towel.

❽ Mark uses an electric slicer to cut his bread thinly and evenly; Kerri uses a long, wide serrated knife.

❾ In the rare cases you haven't finished eating it by, say, the third day, you can wrap what's left in parchment paper and put it in an airtight container in the fridge, where it'll be fine (though soft-crusted) for several days more. Or use it to make crumbs or croutons (page 113) or sock it away in the freezer until you have enough for Crumby Cookies (page 225).

To freeze whole or partial loaves, wrap them in parchment paper or plastic and put them in an airtight container; freeze for up to 2 months. Thaw in the refrigerator or wrap loosely in foil and warm in a 300°F oven for about 30 minutes.

Variations

Bittman Bread with Seeds

In Step Three when you add the salt, mix in up to 50 grams any seeds.

- We say 50 grams, but you can push the quantity to 100 grams once you get the hang of things. Mark likes to keep a mixture of seeds—usually caraway, fennel, poppy, and sesame—in a jar. Sunflower, hemp, cumin, nigella, and pepita (pumpkin seed) are some other options; just be mindful of the flavor intensity and combinations before going nuts with the seeds.

Bittman Bread with Cracked Wheat

When you make the jumpstarter in Step One, soak 50 grams cracked wheat in cold water to cover by at least an inch. In Step Two, drain the cracked wheat in a strainer set over a small bowl; include some or all of the soaking liquid when you add water to the dough. Fold the grains in with the flour and proceed with the recipe. You'll probably need to add less water during the folds than you do when making the main recipe.

- We've used all sorts of cracked whole grains here: cracked wheat berries; rye; ancient wheat like farro, einkorn, or spelt; corn; buckwheat; and barley. If you don't have a mill, try pulsing whole kernels in a strong blender or food processor, or buy cracked wheat or rye, steel-cut oats, freekeh (roasted green wheat), or bulgur (presoaked and dried cracked wheat, which means it will be softer after soaking and baking than the other grains).

Bittman Bread with Other Flours

When you make the dough in Step Two, use another grain, legume, or nut flour to replace 30 to 50 grams of the wheat flour. During the folds, watch the dough closely: Some flours will absorb more water than wheat, but most will take less. Before slashing the loaf, dust the top with some of the flour you used in the dough.

● The dough takes to minor spins easily so go ahead and try whatever you like. Barley is an ancient and very good addition; buckwheat lends beautiful color and great flavor; rye is so good it gets its own treatment (see pages 103, 108, and 121). But try any other flour: corn, chickpea, farro, fava, oat, almond, or any ground whole grain or legume you'd use for cooking.

Bittman Bread with Oats

When you make the dough in Step Two, replace 25 grams of the flour with 75 grams rolled oats. (Not instant, please. But if you want to use steel-cut oats, follow the directions for the cracked wheat variation above.) Increase the first addition of water in that step to 130 grams. After slashing the loaf before baking, scatter a fistful of oats on top.

● One of Kerri's favorites. In the crumb, the oats become soft and on top they're a little crunchy. You'll probably add a little more water than usual during folding since the oats absorb water.

Bittman Bread with Millet or Quinoa

When you make the jumpstarter in Step One, soak 40 grams millet or quinoa in 125 grams cold water in a small bowl. In Step Two, drain the now plumped grains in a strainer set over a small bowl. Include some or all of the soaking liquid when you add water to the dough. Reserve a spoonful of the soaked grains for the top of the loaf if you like, and add the rest when you mix the dough.

- Soaked millet or quinoa brings lovely texture to the bread (not at all gritty). Scattering the reserved grain over the top of the loaf just before slashing and baking is decorative and adds a toasty flavor and crunch, but you can always just mix it all into the dough.

Bittman Bread with Dried Fruit and Nuts

When you add the salt in Step Three, mix in up to 50 grams each dried fruit and nuts to make a classic walnut-raisin or date-nut.

- Use any combination of dried fruit (raisins, cherries, dates, or apricots) and nuts (walnuts, pecans, almonds, pistachios, or even peanuts). Chop them as necessary but not too small; you can crumble walnuts or pecans with your hands. Mark likes to add 1 teaspoon cinnamon or cardamom to the dough, too, and about 75 grams (¼ cup) honey or maple syrup, added along with the salt, is also nice.

Bittman Bread with Cheese

When you add the salt in Step Three, fold in anywhere from 100 to 150 grams grated cheese. Fold and bake as usual.

- Exactly how much to add depends on how strong the cheese is and how much of it you want to taste. Hard or semisoft cheeses work best, since they add flavor without gumming up the interior crumb. Try cheddar, Parmesan, Romano, Manchego, Gruyère, or Emmental.

Mostly White Sourdough Bread

Make the jumpstarter as directed in Step One. In Step Two, substitute all-purpose white or bread flour for the whole wheat. (Or go 50/50 white and whole wheat.) You probably won't need too much more water during folds, just enough to keep the dough from sticking to your hands.

- This will be like the country-style or *levain* loaves from your favorite bakery, with just a hint of whole wheat. We almost always prefer all whole wheat, but it's a gorgeous loaf and those who haven't fully bought into our quest take to it well.

Big Bittman Bread

Simply double the recipe and use a 4½- or 5-quart pot for baking. Everything else stays the same.

● A showstopping loaf for family dinners or gifting. It works well with the basic recipe or any of the variations.

---

7 Additions to Bittman Bread

These are just a few easy ideas; scattered throughout the book you'll find complete recipes for turning the basic bread into bold new twists on familiar favorites, with loads of other sweet and savory ingredients. Mix in any of the following ingredients when you add the salt in Step Three. We've given you suggested quantities for the lighter things like spices in volume measurements instead of grams.

1. Pitted olives, chopped into big pieces (up to 100 grams)

2. Chopped nuts or seeds (up to 100 grams)

3. Chopped fresh rosemary or lavender leaves (1 to 2 tablespoons)

4. Cracked black pepper (up to 1 tablespoon)

5. Saffron threads (just a pinch, crumbled between your fingers)

6. Ground cinnamon (up to 1 teaspoon)

7. Ground cardamom (up to ½ teaspoon)

Reading the Dough

Our bread-making process doesn't entail a lot of actual work, so your main job is to pay attention to what the dough tells you. In order to read your dough—and by that we mean recognizing what its physical characteristics are communicating—you need to know some vocabulary. Bread making has a language all its own (see the Glossary on page 46), and sourdough is a dialect. Following the detailed side notes in the Bittman Bread recipe will also help.

The ultimate goal is to know when dough is ready to bake and what it needs to get there. (The baking itself, assuming a reliable oven, is a no-brainer.) You're working toward a dough that's strong and elastic—meaning you can pull and stretch it without it easily breaking—so that it can trap the gas and steam that will be created during fermentation and baking.

ABOUT ADDING WATER

Probably the biggest challenge is judging the right amount of water to add during the folds; that water is what will get your dough to the right level of strength and elasticity. We give amounts, of course, but how much you need may vary based on the flour, the temperature, the humidity, and some other factors. When mixing the dough, you want all traces of dry flour to be gone; that's easy.

More judgment is needed during the folds, especially the first one: You want to add not only enough water to keep your hands from sticking, but to create a sheen on the dough's surface, even if it's still a little shaggy. Once you see some sheen on the dough, take that as a signal to proceed with caution. Adding more water turns that sheen into a milky coating on the surface of the dough—which can be okay unless that milkiness turns from a coating to a puddle that doesn't easily reabsorb into the dough. Wet your hands just enough to keep the dough from sticking during folds; at some point you might not even need to wet them at all.

WATCH FOR SPRINGINESS AND WEBBING

As the folds progress, the dough will start to scream "I'm alive." (This is really a fun and incredible thing, and you'll see it on your first try.) You're looking for spring, liveliness, and maybe a few visible air bubbles. The dough should literally move—almost like it's breathing—after you handle it and set it back down.

Another sign of strength and elasticity is webbing. The dough will show visible strands much like Silly Putty, stretchy socks, or rubber cement. Try pulling and stretching a pinch between the thumb and first two fingers of both hands: You'll be able to stretch these strands apart a couple of inches in different directions. If you can't, then the dough isn't quite ready for shaping. (Or you're not using a flour that doesn't easily develop elasticity and strength; see page 34.)

The traditional test that properly fermented dough is ready for baking is to press a wet finger into it and watch what happens to the indent; it should spring back a little. If it springs back a lot, wait a few minutes; if it doesn't spring back at all, check sooner next time. You're going to start baking in a cold oven and you want that dough to be lively, since it will finish rising as the oven heats. But if you wait too long to bake, it's not visibly lively anymore; the dough has overproofed and will begin to collapse and slacken.

Smell is an excellent indicator, too. As the fermentation progresses, the dough's scent will mellow a bit and begin to be less like starter and more like bread.

CHANGES AS THE DOUGH BAKES

How your dough behaves in the oven is similarly variable, thus the broad time ranges and visual cues in many recipes. As you bake more loaves, you'll develop your own tastes—for a dark or light crust, for example—and you'll be able to make adjustments. One tip worth mentioning here: After the bread bakes directly on the rack for a few minutes, you might want to shut off the oven and let the crust get even crunchier. We both do that sometimes, but the timing and results are so nuanced it's impossible to give directions other than to say "try it." (We talk a little more about this on page 73.)

All these traits will develop over time in the presence of water, warmth, and handling. Factors like the temperature of your fridge and kitchen and the time since you last fed the starter, as well as knowing when to add water and how long to let the dough sit in the pot before baking, are all going to affect the way you make bread on any given day. That's why the timing and measurements in the recipe are guidelines, not rules.

HOW TO SUBSTITUTE WHITE FLOUR

As you know by now, we believe there's little reason to make white bread, but we do so in a pinch—or moments of weakness. (Mark insists on confirming that as of this writing, he has not made a white bread in more than two years, except for an occasional pizza. Kerri came around more slowly, but until she made the breads photographed for this book, she had gone a full year exclusively on whole grain.)

You might surprise yourself: Our technique makes amazing white bread, definitely a notch or two above the no-knead recipe Mark helped popularize around 2006. But we're hopeful you won't make a habit of it.

Use your regular starter (or if you like, make an all-white starter), and replace all or some of the whole wheat flour in any of the recipes in this book with white all-purpose or bread flour. (For the sweets, stick with all-purpose.) Cut the water by 25 percent to start, then add more during folding if the dough remains too stiff. Bread flour should get you a little more strength and elasticity (and hold water pretty well); all-purpose will deliver a more tender crumb and will absorb less water than bread flour.

BAKING BREAD ON ANY SCHEDULE

One astonishing attribute of this bread is the flexibility of its timing during fermentation. You can adjust the process to fit your schedule. The recipe reflects the way we usually do it: Make the jumpstarter before bed, then finish the dough, fold, and bake in the morning. A close second in frequency is to begin in the morning and bake in the late afternoon or evening.

But you can slow this down with the refrigerator—effectively hitting the pause button—and bake almost any time you want. At 40°F in the cool dark, the dough goes into hibernation; it's in a deep sleep but still breathing. You can delay the process by 24 hours, easily, or you can pause for an hour or two, or six, almost whenever you want. You can, for example, make the jumpstarter at night, add the remaining flour in the morning, throw the dough in the fridge, leave the house, and pick it up whenever you get back— even the next day! (Cover it as usual so it doesn't dry out.)

In fact, *any* time you need to take a break from the process—after you make the jumpstarter or dough, in between folds, or just before baking—simply put the covered bowl in the refrigerator. Up to 12 hours is almost always fine. (The exception is after the last fold, when we don't recommend pushing the time at all.) You can even put it in the refrigerator, take it out for a while, and put it back in.

Once you pull the dough out of the fridge, give it a little time to warm up and resume signs of activity before proceeding. In our experience, the bread develops more flavor and actually performs better after hibernating, which professional bakers call "retarding the dough." You might find yourself adding a little more water during folds, and your resulting crumb might be a tad tighter— not necessarily a bad thing.

You can also speed things up with a few shortcuts, some with little noticeable downside. Mark has great success shortening the time the dough rests after Step Two, before adding salt (he usually does 45 minutes)—and also cutting the time between folds to 25 minutes. (When in a hurry, he will even do 15 minutes between folds.) If you shave 15 minutes here and 5 minutes there . . . you can cut the post-mixing time by almost an hour.

When Kerri's need for bread is urgent, she skips the jumpstarter entirely, mixing 100 grams starter with all the remaining ingredients. This she lets sit, either in the fridge or out, for up to 12 hours. After a couple of quick folds, she transfers the dough to the pot or a loaf pan. This shortcut is more like making yeasted bread, and works best for loaf or flat breads, especially if olive oil is involved. The results tend to have a tighter, more uniform crumb but are still very good.

All About Feeding Your Starter

All you really *need* to know about starter is described in the main recipe on page 24 and in the Glossary on page 46. This section is for the curious, for those who want to delve deeper.

If you've ever read anything about starters—or know people who cultivate them—you probably think you know the basics: Maintain a strict protocol of feeding equal parts flour and water to some set amount of starter, discard any extra starter so you can keep accurate measure. Constantly monitor for bubbling. And use regularly.

No, no, no, and sure, yeah. If you're not using your starter regularly, what do you want it for? Feeding our way takes almost no work. In fact, once your starter is alive, you'll maintain it in less than a minute every time you make a jumpstarter. As long as you do that at least once a week, you don't need to think about much else. Starter is easier to keep alive than many houseplants.

Understandably, people become obsessed by starter. But really, we recommend you ignore the angst. Our way of working with sourdough starter requires a minimum of maintenance and zero fretting. Bread making should be rewarding, not punishing.

FEEDING BASICS

We've simplified matters without sacrificing quality. Since we believe in neither throwing food away nor forcing ourselves to eat pancakes just to use up some of our starter, we *never* discard. (By all means, if you want to make pancakes, make pancakes; see page 203.) If you maintain 250 grams of starter in the refrigerator you'll always have enough to bake anything in the book, even a couple of things in a single day. That's the first advantage to our method.

(clockwise, from top left)
Here's what a whole wheat starter looks like after feeding and sitting at room temperature for 30 minutes or so. You can see bubbling and puffing.

Here's what the same starter looks like right after it comes out of the fridge. This one has been in there almost a week so it's compact, not poofy like those that have only been in a day or two might be, though there are still small bubbles.

Sometimes starters separate and dark liquid pools on top, especially if they've been in the fridge more than a week without feeding or sat out on the counter for a day or more. As long as there are still some bubbles and it only smells like yeast or alcohol—never ammonia—it should be fine. Just stir and feed it.

The second "trick" is our jumpstarter, which uses the same amount of starter (100 grams) for Bittman Bread—and most of the other recipes in the book—every time you bake. And not coincidentally, every time you make a jumpstarter, you feed the remaining starter with the same amount (again, 100 grams), in the form of 50 grams each of water and flour. In recipes that call for more starter, you simply replace it at the same 50/50 ratio, regardless of the total used. So if you take out 150 grams for pizza, you'd feed the starter 75 grams each flour and water.

The starter will stay alive for a long, long time in the refrigerator, weeks—and even, if you're willing to work a bit to revive it, months. (We tell how Kerri reanimated her long-frozen Frankenstarter below.) But although the starter might not die if you starve it, it won't thrive either. That's why we recommend feeding whenever you make a loaf of bread, or at least weekly.

STARTER NOTES FOR ENTHUSIASTS

Once you get comfortable keeping the starter going, you'll probably want to explore some nuances. Having an active starter in your fridge is the best way to ensure that you're going to get a lively dough.

You can, as an extra bit of insurance, make what we call a "superstarter," by feeding your starter a few hours before you make the jumpstarter, then making an exception to our usual rule of refrigerating it, and leaving it at room temperature. This guarantees the freshest, liveliest starter possible, just below its peak leavening power. (What professional bakers call a "young" starter.)

Using superstarter in the jumpstarter—as opposed to starter that may have been in the fridge a week—adds some extra spring and lift in the oven, enough to top out in the 2-quart pot. But honestly? We almost never do it unless we think our starter is fading or we're trying to revive it. Again, feed and bake at least weekly and you'll never have to worry about it.

Within limits, starter composition, and therefore consistency, is up to you; if you like a drier starter, that's fine—we happen to like wetter (see the photos on page 95), so often use 60% water and 40% flour. It's a tad less acidic, a little more bubbly—and simply more convenient because it's pourable. You might try it and if you don't like it, revert to 50/50. But remember you're going to adjust the water content in the bread itself during folding anyway.

Many people use rye in their starter and, flavor-wise, it's a nice addition. Even if your dough is all-wheat, you'll get a strong hint of rye flavor, which most people like. But even a little rye makes your dough gummier and less elastic, because rye contains way less gluten than wheat. So we use whole wheat starters all the time, because they perform better, even in rye breads.

Starter is flexible, and even can be preserved longer-term. And, even though it's easy to create anew, you might want to try to keep a beloved aged starter, or one you were given as a gift. Kerri froze her original starter for a year, then recently thawed it overnight it the fridge and fed it for three days at room temperature. It recovered. (She dubbed it "Frankenstarter.") People have also had success dehydrating starter in thin sheets, which makes it convenient for mailing.

(clockwise, from top left)
Stiff starter: When the starter is about 50%/50% water/flour—meaning it's 100% hydrated—it looks like this.

Spoonable starter: Add an extra 10 to 20% water during feeding—so 5 to 10 grams for every 50 grams—and it thins a little more.

We try to keep our starter at least spoonable, sometimes even pourable like this, which means if the starter is stiff you could be adding closer to 50% more water (an extra 25 grams) during a regular 50-gram feeding.

Is Wetter Better?

MB:

I thought we agreed not to talk about hydration.

KC:

We did. The word—which is the ratio of water to flour, expressed as a percentage, and has become a crucial part of many conversations among serious bakers—is explained in our Glossary on page 46. But we do need to chat about the importance of water in whole grain breads.

MB:

Right. The most important thing to know is that real whole grain flours contain all the parts of the kernel, including all the germ and bran, and that those particles absorb a lot of water. So in order for whole grain breads to get lift and develop strength and elasticity, the dough must be wetter than (probably) any bread dough you've ever made. It's got almost as much water as flour!

KC:

Yes, sometimes I push water content—okay: hydration—to the extreme. So let's provide some solid advice on the topic: We've found that the range for most flours is 85% to 95% water to flour. (100% hydration means equal amounts, by weight, of water and flour.) But you don't have to do the math. Follow the directions and visual cues in the formula and photos here and you'll find your sweet spot.

MB:

Still, it's worth explaining how to find the amount of water that lets the strength of the flour overcome the weight of the bran and germ while promoting webbing and spring. There are visual and tactile cues that, once you've made a few breads, you'll rarely miss, even if you change flour or try a new variation.

KC:

Maybe it seems obvious, but it took a while for me to learn that the flour and water must come together at the beginning. Lumpy soup is almost impossible to revive, because it dilutes the yeasts' activity. Better to start with a dough that's just wet enough—you should never see unmixed flour—and build in more water during the first couple of folds.

MB:

Watching for that dough to develop the first sign of milkiness is key. The second you see a little water leaching out of the dough, a bit of liquid that the dough isn't absorbing right away—stop. That's enough water. And if the dough starts to break down at all, bits come flying off, or it begins to sort of tear on the surface—that's an overhydrated dough. It will probably still come together nicely, but it's time for you to stop adding water. And adding flour really only makes matters worse.

KC:

Learn by doing. Familiarity breeds confidence.

Rich Sandwich Bread, page 125

CHAPTER 4

BEYOND THE BASICS

Rye breads, sandwich loaves, and yes, even baguettes

Mark's Rye, page 103

EVEN BEFORE WE'D FINALIZED the basic Bittman Bread recipe, we were trying the techniques with different flours, added ingredients, and other classic loaves. We needed to discover just how far we could go, how flexible our method was and the variety of situations to which it would adapt, and what we might learn that would improve the basic bread.

What we realized over weeks and months is what people discovered at least 10,000 years ago: Natural starter is the best foundation for every whole grain baked good, from roti-like flatbread to baguettes, from sweet or savory pancakes to sandwich bread. We found that everything we imagined could be adapted to this technique, using 100 percent whole grains and the same starter.

This chapter is largely devoted to a handful of the loaves Americans love most (or should!). Mark is particularly keen on rye breads, so there are several different options included here. His favorite is inspired by the bakery rye of his childhood, but he's also worked on a classic Scandinavian-style rye—the signature tight-crumbed kind often sliced paper-thin for open-face sandwiches. A variation of Kerri's Sandwich Loaf also features rye.

There's a revelatory rich brioche- or challah-style bread, golden with eggs, milk, and lots of butter, baked in a pan like a classic sandwich loaf, with variations for a boule and dinner rolls.

Finally, there are baguettes, a challenge for sure. Neither of us had ever had a whole wheat version we'd want to make a second time, and we doubted that this mountain could be climbed. Kerri went after the challenge with zeal that verged on obsession. Turns out the starter—and a few sheets of foil—put the grail in reach.

If you're like us, your enthusiasm will probably leave you with leftover bread. So this chapter also has a section of ideas for turning bits and pieces into the usual crumbs and croutons, as well as unexpected things like porridge and migas.

Mark's Rye

When I (Mark) was growing up in New York City, my mom regularly sent me to Craig's Bakery on First Avenue near 20th Street for a loaf of rye. The crust was really good—thin, crisp, and stretchy; the bread could be bought with or without caraway seeds. My guess is that it was 10 or 20 percent rye (as you'll see, that's plenty to change both flavor and texture) and the rest white flour, which meant the crumb was mushy and moist. I often ate a quarter of a loaf between Craig's and home.

Sixty years have gone by. This bread is both the ancestor and the descendant of Craig's rye, which was made at a time when white flour was in everything. Now we make it as it was undoubtedly made in nineteenth-century Europe, with 100 percent whole grain in both the starter and the dough. The crumb is light, slightly chewy, and with some heft; the crust still crackles.

Since rye doesn't have as much gluten as wheat, the flour won't absorb water and become elastic the same way as all-wheat bread. Too much water causes the texture to become gummy, so keep water to a minimum—just enough to prevent sticking—as you wet your hands and fold the dough. The dough may be soft, but as long as it's not too wet, you will produce a loaf that will dome almost to the top of the pot—a beauty.

As for the caraway seeds: They're optional, but Mark uses a lot, at least half a standard spice jar. If you like that style, buy the seeds by the pound.

continued →

Makes

1 loaf (12 to 14 ½-inch slices)

Time

8 to 12 hours for the
jumpstarter

About 3 hours intermittent
activity to mix and fold the
dough

About 90 minutes
intermittent activity to
shape, rest, and bake
the loaf

INGREDIENTS

**100 grams whole wheat
starter**

**270 grams whole wheat
flour, plus 50 grams for
feeding the starter**

**210 grams water, plus
50 grams for feeding the
starter and more as needed
for folding**

**30 grams whole grain rye
flour, plus more for dusting
the top (optional)**

7 grams salt, or to taste

**25 grams caraway seeds
plus more for the top
(optional)**

**Coarse salt for topping
(optional)**

1. Combine the starter, 100 grams of the whole wheat
flour, and 100 grams of the water in a large bowl to make
the jumpstarter. Stir, scraping the sides and bottom as
necessary, until all the flour is absorbed. Cover with plastic
or a damp kitchen towel and let it sit at room temperature
for 8 to 12 hours. The jumpstarter will bubble and become
quite fragrant. (The timing is flexible to fit your schedule; see
"Baking Bread on Any Schedule" on page 89.) Meanwhile,
feed the remaining starter: Add 50 grams each whole wheat
flour and water and stir or shake. Cover and return the
starter to the refrigerator.

2. When you're ready to make the dough, add the remaining
170 grams whole wheat flour, the 30 grams rye flour, and
110 grams water to the jumpstarter. Stir with a rubber
spatula or your wet hands until a dough forms and looks
springy, 1 to 2 minutes. If there's still flour not incorporated
around the bottom or edges of the bowl, stir in more water
a dribble at a time as you work. The dough should be wet
and shaggy but will form a loose ball. Cover and let it sit for
about 1 hour.

continued →

3. With wet hands, fold the salt and caraway seeds, if you're using them, into the dough, adding just enough water to prevent stickiness. Cover again and let sit about 30 minutes.

4. Proceed with the four folds as described on page 64, at 30-minute (or so) intervals. As you work, wet your hands and if necessary your work surface with just enough water to keep the dough from sticking. This dough won't absorb water the same way as the basic loaf, so be prudent; you don't want the dough to become shaggy and loose. Sometime over the course of the folds, line a 2-quart ovenproof pot with a lid with a sheet of parchment paper, pressing it into the bottom and creasing over the lip to keep it in place.

5. After the fourth fold, wet your hands one final time. Lift the dough ball, cupping your fingers under the bottom, and lower it into the center of the parchment paper–lined pot. Cover the pot with plastic or a damp kitchen towel and let it sit until the dough puffs a bit and an indent made with your finger springs back slowly, 15 to 30 minutes.

6. Dust the top of the dough with rye flour and/or a sprinkling of caraway seeds if you like and slash it with a couple of parallel lines. (Mark sometimes sprinkles coarse salt on top too.) Cover the pot with its lid, put it in a cold oven, and set the heat to 485°F. After 30 minutes, carefully remove the lid. Return the pot to the oven.

7. After another 15 minutes, turn the heat down to 400°F. Remove the pot from the oven and carefully take the loaf off the parchment and put it directly on the rack (or on a pizza stone if you keep one in your oven). Bake until the crust is dark and an instant-read thermometer inserted into the center registers about 205°F, about 30 minutes. Transfer the bread to a wire rack. Cool completely before slicing.

Super Rye

This will be slightly denser, with a tad less doming, especially if the flour you're using doesn't develop good elasticity or strength. But it's so rye-y that true enthusiasts like Mark's friend and neighbor Danny—an unofficial tester over the years—will be happy to make the tradeoff. In Step 2, increase the rye in the dough to 50 grams and reduce the whole wheat to 150 grams. Be extra careful not to oversaturate the dough with water during the folds. Everything else remains the same.

Onion Rye

Use the main recipe. When you add the salt in Step 3, fold in 50 grams chopped onions (½ medium or one small) and reduce the caraway to 20 grams if using.

Cornmeal-Rye Bread with Molasses

A cross between Portuguese broa and an early American cornmeal-molasses bread. The resulting loaf has a chocolaty, stout-like flavor balanced by subtle sweetness. The rye and cornmeal make the texture interesting, too, especially if you use a heavy hand dusting the top of the loaf before baking. Expect the dough to be wetter and less elastic than most other Bittman Bread recipes; in fact, your folds will be more like rolling or wet-handed kneading. The range of water you'll add during the folding process can vary quite a bit, depending on how much moisture your dough can absorb without entirely losing all structure. So be conservative until you get a feel for the dough.

Makes

1 loaf (12 to 14 ½-inch slices)

Time

8 to 12 hours for the jumpstarter

About 3 hours intermittent activity to mix and fold the dough

About 90 minutes intermittent activity to shape, rest, and bake the loaf

continued →

INGREDIENTS

**50 grams fine- or medium-
grind cornmeal, plus more
for dusting the top**

75 grams boiling water

**100 grams whole wheat
starter**

**220 grams whole wheat
flour, plus 50 grams for
feeding the starter**

**175 grams water, plus 50
grams for feeding the
starter and more as needed
for folding**

25 grams molasses

**30 grams whole grain rye
flour, plus more for dusting
the top**

5 grams salt

1. Put the cornmeal and boiling water in a large bowl and stir to combine, scraping any bits from the sides to make a wet lump of mush. Soak for 1 hour.

2. Add the starter to the bowl along with 100 grams of the whole wheat flour and 100 grams of the water to make the jumpstarter. Stir, scraping the sides and bottom as necessary, until all the flour is absorbed. The mixture will be quite wet. Cover with plastic or a damp kitchen towel and let it sit at room temperature for 8 to 12 hours. The jumpstarter will bubble and become quite fragrant. (The timing is flexible to fit your schedule; see "Baking Bread on Any Schedule" on page 89.) Meanwhile, feed the remaining starter: Add 50 grams each whole wheat flour and water and stir or shake. Cover and return it to the refrigerator.

3. When you're ready to make the dough, dissolve the molasses in the remaining 75 grams water in a small bowl; add it to the jumpstarter along with the remaining 120 grams whole wheat flour and the 30 grams rye flour. Stir with a rubber spatula or your wet hands until a shaggy dough forms, 1 to 2 minutes. If there's still flour not incorporated around the bottom or edges of the bowl, stir in more water a dribble at a time as you work. The dough should be wet but will form a loose ball. Cover and let it sit for about 1 hour.

4. With wet hands, fold the salt into the dough, adding just enough water, a few drops at time, to prevent stickiness. Cover again and let sit about 30 minutes.

5. Proceed with the four folds as described on page 64, at 30-minute (or so) intervals. As you work, wet your hands and if necessary your work surface with just enough water to keep the dough from sticking. This dough won't absorb water the same way as the basic loaf, so be prudent; you don't want the dough to become shaggy and loose. Sometime over the course of the folds, line a 2-quart ovenproof pot with a lid pot with a sheet of parchment paper, pressing it into the bottom and creasing over the lip to keep it in place.

6. After the fourth fold, wet your hands one final time. Lift the dough ball, cupping your fingers under the bottom, and lower it into the center of the parchment paper–lined pot. Cover the pot with plastic or a damp kitchen towel and let it sit until the dough puffs a bit and an indent made with your finger springs back slowly, 15 to 30 minutes.

7. Dust the top of the dough generously with a combination of cornmeal and rye flour, but don't slash it. Cover the pot with its lid, put it in a cold oven, and set the heat to 485°F. After 30 minutes, carefully remove the lid. Return the pot to the oven.

8. After another 15 minutes, turn the heat down to 400°F. Remove the pot from the oven and carefully take the loaf off the parchment and put it directly on the rack (or a pizza stone if you keep one in your oven). Bake until the crust starts to crack through the layer of cornmeal and rye and an instant-read thermometer inserted into the center registers about 205°F, about 30 minutes. Transfer the bread to a wire rack. Cool completely, then tap the bottom of the loaf to shake off the extra dust, and slice.

Bread Crumbs

Lots of Ideas for Leftover Bread

You won't waste a crumb of any of the loaves in this chapter—or anywhere in the book—with these second-use recipes. The best tip is to sock away bits and pieces in an airtight container in the freezer. Or you might find yourself baking a designated loaf just for one of the following ideas, or for the cookies on page 225.

Croutons

The classic. Keep them small so they don't get too hard. Spread cubed bread on a rimmed baking sheet and bake in a 250°F oven until firm and crisp, 30 to 60 minutes depending on the size of the cubes and the age of the bread. Or pour a thin film of olive oil in a large skillet and fry the cubes over medium heat, tossing frequently, until crisp on all sides. Either way, store in an airtight container at room temperature. Oven-dried croutons will keep for a month; the fried kind for about a week.

Bread Crumbs

With their pleasantly rich flavor, whole grain breads make crumbs that can taste like cheese or bacon when salted, or like caramel when sweetened. First cut or tear 1-inch pieces. Dry the bread by letting it stand out for a day or two, then pulverize in a food processor or blender, as fine or coarse as you like. You can store the crumbs in a jar in the pantry for months to use for dredging, breading, or making stuffing. Or fry them in hot butter or oil to use as a garnish for salads, vegetables, soups, or simply cooked fish, poultry, or meat.

Melba Toast or Rusks

Slice the bread about ¼ inch thick for Melba toast, ¾ inch thick for rusks. Spread the pieces in an even layer on a baking sheet and dry in a 250°F oven until firm and crisp, 30 to 60 minutes. Both keep for months in an airtight container. Super-crisp Melba toast is perfect for soft cheeses, nut butters, and fruit compotes. Like biscotti, rusks (which take longer to dry) may require dunking or soaking to eat without effort; they're perfect for floating in a bowl of soup. Or put in a shallow bowl of hot milk (or milk and coffee) and drizzle with honey.

Crackers

Since Mark has a mechanical slicer, he does this, too—an idea shared by Renee Erickson, chef and co-owner of Sea Creatures Restaurants in the Pacific Northwest, and a friend of this book's photographer, Jim Henkens. Shave the bread as thinly and carefully as possible on the slicer—⅛ inch is about right; you'll be able to see through it. You can brush the slices with butter or olive oil before toasting if you like but it's not necessary. Spread the crackers out on a large baking sheet and bake in a 400°F oven until browned on both sides, 5 to 10 minutes.

Bread Porridge

This Scandinavian dish is easy to spin in many different directions, and you'll be shocked how good it is. All you do is treat leftover bread like it's cooked grains—which, of course, it is. Tear or cut the bread into smaller-than-bite-size pieces and put in a pot with enough water to cover, or use another liquid like orange juice, cider, milk, beer, or stock. Bring to a boil; reduce the heat and cook, stirring occasionally, until the porridge thickens and the bread breaks apart. Finish with sweet toppings like butter, syrup or honey, applesauce, dried fruit, or nuts. Or go savory with olive oil, salsa, soy sauce, chopped cooked or pickled vegetables, shredded cabbage, or frozen peas or corn.

Migas

Iberia's creative and clever way to turn bread crumbs into a meal. (*Migas* means crumbs.) Take about 8 slices of stale bread, soak them in water to cover just until soft, then wring gently in a clean kitchen towel until dry. Put at least ¼ cup of olive oil in a skillet, add about ½ pound of Spanish chorizo (the dry, cured kind), and cook until it's lightly browned. Add at least a couple of cloves' worth of minced garlic and a minute or two later, crumble in the bread. Cook, stirring occasionally, until the bread browns, 10 minutes or so, adding more oil if the mixture seems dry. Season with salt and a lot of pepper and serve immediately. We should mention that this is especially good with a couple of fried eggs on top.

Wet-Bread Stuffing

Kerri's mom had this wonderful technique for stuffing: Cut or tear 1-inch pieces of bread (don't bother to remove the crusts) and dry by letting it stand out for a day or two. Fill a bowl with tap water and add about 2 cups of bread pieces at a time; let them soak until you can squish them in your fist like a sponge but they're not yet disintegrating, just a minute or so. Grab a handful of wet bread and squeeze it between your palms to wring out excess water. Put the bread in a clean bowl and repeat with another handful. When all the bread is done, crumble the pieces between your fingers until it's the texture of clumpy couscous. Use the crumbs in your favorite stuffing recipe. Or sauté celery, onions, and garlic in butter with chopped fresh sage, and when the aromatics are fragrant and soft, stir in the damp bread crumbs. Moisten the stuffing with stock or do like Kerri's mom and bind it with beaten eggs. Transfer to a buttered baking pan or dish and bake at 400°F until the center is firm and a crust forms on the top and sides.

Panzenella

The summertime classic: Chop ripe tomatoes and toss with chunks of stale bread (any bread will work). We like the bread pretty dry; it soaks up more dressing. Add basil and vinaigrette, or simply oil and lemon or vinegar. In other seasons, omit the tomatoes; try kale or escarole ribbons with dried chiles in fall, citrus and nuts in winter, tender spinach or arugula with lemon juice in spring.

Kerri's Sandwich Loaf

You can make a sandwich out of any loaf, but sometimes nothing but the traditional Pullman, made in a loaf pan, will do. Plus, most supermarket "whole wheat" is too much like commercial white bread and generally not even 100 percent whole wheat.

Enter Kerri's Sandwich Loaf, which follows the same mixing, fermentation, and folding procedures as Bittman Bread but increases the amounts of starter, flour, and water by 50 percent to produce a more-than-2-pound, high-domed, loosely crumbed loaf that slices easily, toasts beautifully, and delivers at least six sandwiches. After Kerri cuts a few slices over the course of a couple of days, she wraps whatever's left loosely in parchment paper and moves it to an airtight container in the fridge.

The pans for this are sometimes called either "standard" or "1-pound." To avoid confusion, we give the inch measurements. Use a metal pan; glass will give you a lopsided rise. You can skip the parchment paper lining if you're absolutely confident your pan is nonstick, but smear it generously with butter or good-quality vegetable oil. We almost always opt for parchment, because it takes the stress out of removing the loaf and helps create a pleasantly chewy crust. For a crisper, browner crust, remove the baked loaf from the pan and let it sit in the turned-off oven, directly on the rack, for 10 minutes or so.

continued →

Makes

1 sandwich loaf (12 ¾-inch slices)

Time

8 to 12 hours for the jumpstarter

About 3 hours intermittent activity to mix and fold the dough

About 2 hours intermittent activity to shape and bake the loaf

INGREDIENTS

150 grams whole wheat starter

450 grams whole wheat flour, plus 75 grams for feeding the starter, and more for dusting (optional)

320 grams water, plus 75 grams for feeding the starter and more as needed for folding

11 or 12 grams salt

1. Combine the starter, 150 grams of the whole wheat flour, and 150 grams of the water in a large bowl to make the jumpstarter. Stir, scraping the sides and bottom as necessary until all the flour is absorbed. Cover with plastic or a damp kitchen towel and let it sit at room temperature for 8 to 12 hours. The jumpstarter will bubble and become quite fragrant. (The timing is flexible to fit your schedule; see "Baking Bread on Any Schedule" on page 89.) Meanwhile, feed the remaining starter: Add 75 grams each whole wheat flour and water and stir or shake. Cover and return it to the refrigerator.

2. When you're ready to make the dough, add the remaining 300 grams flour and 170 grams water to the jumpstarter. Stir with a rubber spatula or your wet hands until a dough forms and looks springy, 1 to 2 minutes. If there's still flour not incorporated around the bottom or edges of the bowl, stir in more water 5 grams at a time (about a teaspoon) as you work. The dough should be wet and shaggy but will form a loose ball. Cover again and let it sit for about 1 hour.

3. With wet hands, fold the salt into the dough, adding enough water to create a sheen on the surface without the dough losing the ability to hold a loose shape. Cover and let it sit about 30 minutes.

4. Proceed with the four folds as described on page 64, at 30-minute (or so) intervals. As you work, wet your hands and the dough with enough water so it becomes smooth while still holding some shape. After the third fold, if you're using parchment paper, line an 8½ x 4½ x 2¾-inch metal loaf pan with a 16-inch length of parchment paper, draping it across the edges. Make creases at the bottom and sides to help it stay in place and crimp the ends; it's okay if the ends aren't fully covered with parchment as long as the bottom seam is. Or smear the pan with butter or oil.

5. After the fourth fold, use wet hands to shape the dough in the bowl if it's broad enough or on a wet work surface; use a gentle rolling action to shape the dough into a thick cylinder. Put it in the prepared pan. Use your fingers to quickly but gently dimple the dough and press it evenly in the pan. Cover the pan with plastic or a damp kitchen towel and let it sit until the dough puffs a bit and an indent made with your finger springs back slowly, 15 to 30 minutes. It will rise to within an inch of the top of the pan.

6. Dust the top with flour if you like and slash the dough lengthwise down the center or slightly to one side. Put the pan in a cold oven and set the heat to 350°F. Bake until the slash opens, the top is browned, and an instant-read thermometer inserted in the center of the loaf registers about 205°F, 70 to 80 minutes. If you used parchment, use it to lift the loaf from the pan and transfer it to a wire rack,

continued →

then carefully slip out the parchment. To remove a loaf baked directly in the pan, let it sit for 10 minutes to separate from the sides and bottom, turn it upside down onto the rack, then turn it upright. If it balks, work a butter knife around the edges and try again, rapping on the bottom to loosen it. Cool completely before slicing.

Kerri's Sandwich Rye

Make the jumpstarter as described in the main recipe. When you mix the dough in Step 2, replace 45 grams of the whole wheat flour with rye flour. With the salt in Step 3, add 35 grams caraway seeds if you like. In Step 6 before you slash the loaf, either dust it with rye flour or scatter a fistful of additional caraway seeds on top.

Kerri's Mostly White Sandwich Bread

Because we know you'll want it, at least once in a while. This will produce the best white sandwich loaf ever. Make the jumpstarter as described in the main recipe. When you make the dough in Step 2 replace the whole wheat flour with 300 grams all-purpose or bread flour and reduce the water to 125 grams. You probably won't need to add too much more water during folding. Otherwise everything else remains the same.

Travel Bread

You know that super-seedy, cracked-grain-y, pleasantly tangy rye loaf used for the Scandinavian open-face sandwiches called smørrebrød? This is it. It keeps forever and travels well (thus the name), is incredibly flavorful, and is best sliced thin. Mark's friend, Danish chef and food writer Trine Hahnemann, got him started on it years ago, and this is an adaptation of her recipe.

The dough is quite different from any other in this book, more like seeds and cracked grains held together with a starter-fermented whole wheat batter that resembles a porridge. There's no folding, just mixing and pouring.

You need the seeds here. Mark's mix includes fennel, caraway, sesame, and poppy. Sunflower, flax, cumin, and pepitas (pumpkin seeds) are all good.

Cracked rye can be tough to find, though Maine Grains and other specialty mills sell it online. Mark uses his mill to crack rye berries, but a powerful blender will also work, especially if it has a special container for dry ingredients. (Kerri used a blender to crack the whole Kernza wheat berries shown in the photograph.) If you can't find it or grind your own, just use cracked wheat, freekeh (cracked green wheat), bulgur, or steel-cut oats. Rolled rye or oats pulsed in a food processor are also fine.

Wrapped in parchment and kept in an airtight container, the bread will last in the fridge for at least a week. (To treat leftovers the traditional way and turn them into porridge, see Bread Porridge, page 114.)

continued →

Makes

1 sandwich loaf (16 to 20 very
thin slices)

Time

8 hours for the jumpstarter

A few minutes to mix the
dough

3½ to 4½ hours to rest and
bake the loaf

INGREDIENTS

**100 grams whole wheat
starter**

**375 grams whole grain
rye flour**

**500 grams water, plus
50 grams for feeding the
starter**

**50 grams whole wheat flour
for feeding the starter, plus
more for dusting the top
(optional)**

**250 grams cracked rye
berries, or cracked wheat
or other grains (see the
headnote)**

50 grams mixed seeds

10 grams salt

1. Combine the starter, rye flour, and 375 grams of the water in a large bowl. Stir, scraping the sides and bottom as necessary, until all the flour is absorbed. Cover with plastic or a damp kitchen towel and let it sit at room temperature until the jumpstarter puffs noticeably, about 8 hours. It won't be bubbly like the usual jumpstarters, but will be quite fragrant. (The timing is flexible to fit your schedule; see "Baking Bread on Any Schedule" on page 89.) Meanwhile, feed the remaining starter: Add 50 grams each whole wheat flour and water and stir or shake. Cover and return it to the refrigerator.

2. When you're ready to make the bread, line an 8½ x 4½ x 2¾ inch metal loaf pan with a 16-inch length of parchment paper, draping it across the edges. Make creases at the bottom and sides to help it stay in place.

3. Add the cracked rye to the jumpstarter along with the seeds, salt, and the remaining 125 grams water. Stir with a spoon until a batter-like dough forms, just a minute or 2. Transfer the dough to the prepared pan, scraping the bowl and spreading the dough evenly with a rubber

continued →

spatula. Cover the pan again with plastic or a damp kitchen towel and let it sit at room temperature until the dough puffs toward the rim of the pan or even a little over, 2 to 4 hours.

4. Heat the oven to 350°F. Put the pan in the oven and bake until the bread is browned on top and an instant-read thermometer inserted in the center of the loaf registers about 200°F, 75 to 90 minutes. (The loaf will be flatter on top than the other loaf breads in the book.) Let cool in the pan for about 15 minutes then lift the loaf out, peel off the parchment, and finish cooling completely on a wire rack before slicing.

Rich Sandwich Bread

When you enrich a natural starter with milk, butter, and eggs and sweeten it with honey, the loaf becomes positively brioche-like. Thin slices make perfect toast points for cheeses, pâté, and spreads. Or go thick for decadent sandwiches or the best French toast ever.

Makes

1 sandwich loaf (12 ¾-inch slices)

Time

8 to 12 hours for the jumpstarter

About 4 hours intermittent activity to mix and fold the dough

About 90 minutes to shape, rest, and bake the loaf

INGREDIENTS

150 grams whole wheat starter

150 grams whole milk

450 grams whole wheat flour, plus 75 grams for feeding the starter

100 grams water, plus 75 grams for feeding the starter and more as needed for folding

113 grams butter (1 stick), softened

4 egg yolks

100 grams honey

11 grams salt

1. Combine the starter, milk, and 150 grams of the whole wheat flour in a large bowl to make the jumpstarter. Stir, scraping the sides and bottom as necessary, until all the flour is absorbed. Cover with plastic or a damp kitchen towel and let it sit at room temperature for 8 to 12 hours. The jumpstarter will bubble and become quite fragrant. (The timing is flexible to fit your schedule; see "Baking Bread on Any Schedule" on page 89.) Meanwhile, feed the remaining starter: Add 75 grams each whole wheat flour and water and stir or shake. Cover and return it to the refrigerator.

2. When you're ready to make the dough, add the remaining 300 grams flour and the 100 grams water to the jumpstarter. Fold with a rubber spatula or your wet hands until the dough becomes springy, 1 to 2 minutes. If there's still flour

continued →

not incorporated, mix in more water, 10 grams at a time. The dough at this stage should be just wet enough to hold together. Cover again and let it sit for about 1 hour.

3. Put the butter, 3 of the egg yolks, the honey, and salt in a bowl and beat with a whisk or electric mixer until everything is combined. The mixture will look like scrambled eggs, but don't worry, it's fine. With wet hands, incorporate the butter mixture into the dough, using your fingers to squish the two mixtures together. It will take a little more handling than you're used to, but you shouldn't need to add any more water than what's on your hands to prevent too much sticking. Cover and let it sit about 30 minutes.

4. Proceed with the four folds as described on page 64, at 30-minute (or so) intervals. As you work, wet your hands and the dough with enough water so that it becomes smoother while still holding some shape. Since the dough has so much butter in it, expect it to be a lot wetter and less elastic than the other doughs in this book.

5. After the fourth fold, line an 8½ x 4½ x 2¾-inch metal loaf pan with a 16-inch length of parchment paper, draping it across the edges. Make creases at the bottom and sides to help it stay in place. Use a gentle rolling action to shape the dough into a thick cylinder, transfer it to the pan, then press with your fingertips to fill the corners and spread evenly. Cover and let it sit until it puffs a bit. (This final rise usually takes 15 to 30 minutes but rarely more.) Beat the remaining egg yolk with a few drops water until uniform. Brush most of the egg wash over the top of the loaf and slash the dough lengthwise down the center, or crosswise in 5 places.

continued →

6. Put the pan in a cold oven and set the heat to 350°F. Bake until the top is crisp and browned and an instant-read thermometer inserted into the center registers between 205° and 210°F, about an hour or a little longer. Lift the bread out of the pan, remove the parchment, and put the bread on a wire rack. Cool completely before slicing.

Rich Crusty Bread

For a golden boule—round-shaped bread—with a deeply colored exterior you can adjust this dough to fit in your 2-quart pot as described on page 72. In Step 1, reduce the flour, milk, and starter to 100 grams each to make the jumpstarter. For the dough in Step 2, decrease the amount of flour to 200 grams and water to 75 grams. In Step 3, beat together 2 egg yolks, 85 grams butter (¾ stick), 70 grams honey, and 7 grams salt. In Step 5, after the fourth fold, form the dough into a ball and, instead of using a loaf pan, put the bread in a parchment paper–lined 2-quart pot with a lid. Cover and let it rest until puffed, 15 to 30 minutes. Slash a large X in the dough. Put the pot in a cold oven, set the heat to 485°F, and bake for 30 minutes. Remove the lid, turn the heat down to 400°F and bake for 10 minutes, no longer or the crust gets too dark. Then transfer the loaf directly to the oven rack, and bake until the internal temperature is between 205° and 210°F, 15 to 30 minutes.

Rich Rolls

Follow the main recipe to make 12 rolls. After the fourth fold, pick up at Step 5 of the Garlicky Dinner Rolls recipe on page 162, or use for any of its variations.

Baguettes

Making baguettes is a badge of honor. Even professional chefs who make excellent white flour loaves struggle with getting whole wheat to behave the same way and form a chewy, open crumb and crackling crisp crust.

We're here to say with confidence: "You can do it." This recipe produces a chewy-on-the-inside, crunchy-on-the-outside whole wheat baguette. In fact, just about everything is the same as the basic bread until shaping. At that point, the trick is to make your own molds and start the loaves, tented with foil, in a cold oven. The how-to photos on page 132 will make it easy. Whether you slice them on the bias or split them to make Parisian-style sandwiches, everyone will be amazed.

Makes

2 baguettes (4 to 6 servings)

Time

8 to 12 hours for the jumpstarter

About 3 hours intermittent activity to mix and fold the dough

About 1¾ hours to shape, rest, and bake the baguettes

continued →

INGREDIENTS

100 grams whole wheat starter

300 grams whole wheat flour, plus 50 grams for feeding the starter and more for dusting

210 grams water, plus 50 grams for feeding the starter and more as needed for folding

7 grams salt, or to taste

1. Combine the starter, 100 grams of the whole wheat flour, and 100 grams of the water in a large bowl to make the jumpstarter. Stir, scraping the sides and bottom as necessary, until all the flour is absorbed. Cover with plastic or a damp kitchen towel and let it sit at room temperature for 8 to 12 hours. The jumpstarter will bubble and become quite fragrant. (The timing is flexible to fit your schedule; see "Baking Bread on Any Schedule" on page 89.) Meanwhile, feed the remaining starter: Add 50 grams each whole wheat flour and water and stir or shake. Cover and return it to the refrigerator.

2. When you're ready to make the dough, add the remaining 200 grams flour and 110 grams water to the jumpstarter. Stir with a rubber spatula or your wet hands until a dough forms and looks springy, 1 to 2 minutes. If there's still flour not incorporated around the bottom or edges of the bowl, stir in more water 5 grams (about a teaspoon) at a time as you work. The dough should be wet and shaggy but will form a loose ball. Cover again and let it sit for about 1 hour.

3. With wet hands, fold the salt into the dough, adding enough water to create a sheen on the surface without the dough losing its ability to hold a loose shape. Cover and let it sit about 30 minutes.

4. Proceed with the four folds as described on page 64, at 30-minute (or so) intervals. As you work, wet your hands and the dough with enough water so it becomes smooth while still holding some shape. After the third fold, make molds by cutting two sheets of foil, each about 18 x 12 inches. Crimp each lengthwise into a cradle about 3 inches

continued →

(top) To hold the dough in shape, you'll make two cradles by crimping big sheets of foil and lining each with parchment. The dough won't quite fill them at first.

(center) After resting, the dough should fill the cradles better. Dust the tops with flour before slashing if you'd like.

(bottom) You'll also need to make a tent for baking the baguettes. If you fold the edges of two sheets together a couple times the seam with be tight and you'll have almost double the usual size. Then make a perpendicular fold across the center of the fused sheets. Crimp the edges of foil around the pan, lifting the center of the foil as you work to give the baguettes some head room.

wide, and line each with a sheet of parchment paper (see the photos on page 132). Set them up on a baking sheet.

5. After the fourth fold, divide the dough in half. Gently stretch one half to fit in a mold and lay it on the parchment. Repeat with the other loaf. Cover with plastic or a damp kitchen towel and let them sit until the dough puffs a bit and an indent made with your finger doesn't spring back all the way, 30 to 60 minutes. Dust the tops with flour and slash each loaf across at a diagonal in 4 places.

6. To bake, make a foil tent by cutting two pieces of foil at least 18 inches long. Stack the foil pieces, grab both along one long edge, and fold about ½ inch over a couple of times to make a center seam so you end up with one big sheet. Make another fold perpendicular to the seam so that there's a peak you can tug on to give the loaves some headroom as they bake. Fit the tent over the pan, tuck the edges underneath, and pinch tightly on all four sides of the pan. Pull up gently on the peak to make a foil tent over the pan.

One Big Po'Boy Loaf

You'll need a large baking sheet (rimmed or unrimmed)—figure 18 x 14 inches. Instead of two 18-inch-long, 3-inch-wide foil cradles, make one that's about 4 inches wide, and line it with parchment. Put it diagonally across the pan. After the fourth fold, shape the dough into a single loaf. Cover with the foil tent as described. The baking time should be about the same as for two loaves.

7. Put the whole rig in a cold oven and set the heat to 485°F. After 30 minutes, carefully remove the foil tent so the steam wafts away from you. Turn the heat down to 400°F and put the pan back in the oven for 15 minutes; the loaves should be set and turning golden. Remove the baguettes from the foil and parchment and put them directly on the rack. Bake until an instant-read thermometer inserted into the thickest part of a loaf registers between 200° and 205°F, 10 to 15 minutes. Cool on wire racks before slicing or tearing.

CHAPTER 5

PIZZA, FLAT-BREADS, AND ROLLS

Spins on the classic margherita, focaccia, "American" muffins, knots and crescents, pretzels, biscuits, two skillet breads, and hand pies

I T DIDN'T SURPRISE US THAT MUCH when we extended the basic Bittman Bread recipe to the world of other loaves, but when we started moving into flatbreads and the like, we were amazed at the adaptability our dough displayed.

Not that it was easy. Our first attempts at pizza were particularly far from perfect. Because not only were we looking for world-class results, we wanted a process that was flexible, not frantic. It took the help of our colleague Daniel Meyer and dozens of variations on the method to get the recipe right.

Likewise with whole wheat focaccia which, we felt, should be as light as its white flour counterpart. Both of these now use surprising but not complicated methods.

English muffins (we call them "American Muffins," for reasons we explain) were a no-brainer, since they're made almost exactly the same way they are with white flour.

Similarly, dinner rolls of all shapes and flavors are easily shaped with a knife and a cutting board. Biscuits, too, turn out to be an adaptation rather than a reinvention, and they are fantastic.

Pretzels are the most labor-intensive recipe in the book; there is real work here. But they're not difficult and are extremely forgiving of beginners. They are also instant obsessions.

The two skillet breads could not be more different: The first is cooked quickly in a dry pan on the stove; the other is an oven-baked pancake, with both wild and familiar variations.

A calzone-like hand pie—the only other main dish in the book besides pizza—closes the chapter.

10 Possible Toppings for Pizza

After the cheese, top the pizza with a scattering of one or two of the following, being careful not to overload it:

1. Thinly sliced pepperoni, salami, or prosciutto

2. Anchovies

3. Chopped pitted black olives

4. Grated Parmesan cheese

5. Thinly sliced red onion

6. Roasted bell peppers, cut into strips

7. Thinly sliced cremini mushrooms, tossed in olive oil

8. A handful of arugula or chopped kale, tossed in olive oil

9. Raw eggs (1 per serving; crack on top of other fillings and they will cook during the second baking)

10. Torn basil leaves or chopped parsley, for garnish after baking

Pizza

The trick to whole wheat pizza is to make sure the dough rises, bakes through, *and* develops a crisp, pleasantly chewy crust. We address that by partially baking the pies first with just a smear of deeply flavored homemade tomato paste to set the dough, then topping them and baking them more to finish them. Between the option to hibernate the dough (as you can with almost all of our doughs; see "Baking Bread on Any Schedule" on page 89) and the make-ahead first bake, you can make pizza pretty quickly any night of the week, as long as you plan ahead.

You also have options when it comes to baking vessels. For parbaking you can use a baking sheet, pizza pan, even a cast-iron or carbon-steel skillet. If you have a stone, you'll set the pan on that. After topping, the pies go directly on a heated stone or baking sheet.

The tomato paste takes time but very little attention. It'll come together while you fold the dough. You'll welcome the concentrated flavor, but substitute canned if you want an easier route. In the summer, puree good, ripe tomatoes and reduce the liquid the way we describe here. The results are incredible. (You can make the sauce ahead; transfer it to a container, cover tightly, and refrigerate for up to a few days or freeze for months.)

If you use canned paste, you'll need one 6- to 8-ounce can or jar (or about 1½ tubes). Stir in 15 grams olive oil and 1 clove minced garlic if you like and skip the sauce-making part of Step 5 in the recipe.

Unlike many pizza recipes (including our earlier yeasted white-flour versions, like the one in *How to Cook Everything*), freezing and thawing this

continued →

dough leaves you with a soggy blob that bakes up on the gummy side; better to adjust the timing by refrigerating the dough before, during, or after the folds.

That said, frozen leftover slices reheat in a 400°F oven quite well. Heat them, wrapped in foil, on a baking sheet or stone until they thaw, about 10 minutes. Then remove the foil and let them crisp directly on the surface for a couple of minutes more.

Makes

4 main dish or 8 appetizer servings

Time

8 to 12 hours for the jumpstarter

About 3 hours intermittent activity to mix and fold the dough and make the sauce
About 30 minutes to shape and parbake the pizzas (can be done up to 2 hours ahead of serving)

15 minutes to top and finish baking the pizzas

continued →

INGREDIENTS

150 grams whole wheat starter

450 grams whole wheat flour, plus 75 grams for feeding the starter

300 grams water, plus 75 grams for feeding the starter and more as needed for folding

11 grams salt, plus more for the sauce

Whole garlic cloves (as many as you like, or none at all)

80 grams extra virgin olive oil

1 large can (28 or 29 ounces/ about 800 grams) pureed tomatoes

Pepper

228 grams (8 ounces) mozzarella (any kind)

Additional toppings from the list on page 138 (optional)

1. Combine the starter, 150 grams of the whole wheat flour, and 150 grams of the water in a large bowl to make the jumpstarter. Stir, scraping the sides and bottom until all the flour is absorbed. Cover with plastic or a damp kitchen towel and let it sit at room temperature for 8 to 12 hours. The jumpstarter will bubble and become quite fragrant. (The timing is flexible to fit your schedule; see "Baking Bread on Any Schedule" on page 89.) Meanwhile, feed the remaining starter: Add 75 grams each whole wheat flour and water and stir or shake. Cover and return it to the refrigerator.

2. When you're ready to make the dough, add the remaining 300 grams flour and 150 grams water. Stir with a rubber spatula or your wet hands until a dough forms and looks springy, 1 to 2 minutes. If there's still flour not incorporated around the bottom or edges of the bowl, stir in more water 5 grams (about a teaspoon) at a time as you work. The dough should be wet and shaggy but will form a loose ball. Cover again and let it sit for about 1 hour.

3. With wet hands, fold the salt into the dough, adding enough water to create a sheen on the surface without the dough losing its ability to hold a loose shape. Cover and let it sit about 30 minutes.

4. Proceed with the four folds as described on page 64, at 30-minute (or so) intervals. As you work, wet your hands and the dough with enough just water so that the dough becomes smooth while still holding some shape, but without saturating it. (For pizza you want the dough on the dry side.)

5. After making the first fold, prepare the sauce (or open the canned paste): Peel the garlic if you're using it and smash the cloves with the flat side of a knife. Put 1 tablespoon of the oil in a medium skillet over medium heat, add the garlic, and cook, shaking the pan occasionally, until the garlic turns golden in spots, about 3 minutes. Add the tomatoes and sprinkle with a little salt. (If you're not using the garlic, add the tomatoes to the warm oil.) Bring the sauce to a gentle but steady bubble and cook, stirring occasionally, until most of the liquid evaporates and the sauce darkens, sticks to the bottom of the pan, and becomes a paste, at least an hour and usually closer to 90 minutes. (Don't rush this step; it's important for the sauce to be dry so the dough bakes properly.) Taste the sauce and add more salt if you like, and some pepper; remove the sauce from the heat until you need it for the pizzas. Thinly slice, tear, or grate the cheese and get any other toppings ready.

6. After the third fold, if you're using a pizza stone, put it on a rack in the lower part of the oven. (If you're not using a stone, just arrange the racks so that one is in the lower part.) Heat the oven to 500°F. Generously grease your pizza pans—use four 10-inch individual pans or two 12-inch large ones—or baking sheets (if you don't have pizza pans) with the remaining oil.

7. After the fourth fold, use wet hands to divide the dough into two or four equal pieces; roll them into loose balls. Working with one piece at a time, hold it in the air and let the dough stretch while you work your hands around the edges to shape it into a circle; get it as thin as you can without it tearing, then spread it onto an oiled pan. Wet your hands again and use your fingertips to press the dough into a circle about ¼ inch thick. (That will be about 9 inches in diameter for individual pizzas, or 12 inches for large. If you're using baking sheets, shape the circles so you can fit multiple pies per sheet.)

continued on page 147 →

(clockwise, from top left)
The brightly flavored homemade tomato paste takes up to 90 minutes but not tons of attention. You've got to be nearby for folding the dough anyway, so you may as well put a skillet on the stove. This is how thick it should be.

To begin shaping the dough for pizza: Wet your hands and hold one of the pieces above the greased pan and stretch gently to form a disk. Work your fingers around the perimeter to stretch it as thin as you can, letting gravity do some of the work. If it tears, pinch the hole closed.

When the disk starts to feel out of control, put it in the prepared pan and gently stretch as much as you can in the pan before beginning to press. The dough will probably keep springing back—which is a good sign for future chewiness. Take breaks for a couple minutes to let it rest and soon it will get there.

(clockwise, from top left)
Try not to overwork the dough, which can make it cakey and tough. Pressing with your fingertips serves to dimple, press, and stretch without doing too much of anything. You want the dough to be no more than ½ inch thick. It's okay if it's uneven—you'll get a mix of different textures and crunch, which we love.

Fingers are the easiest tool for dabbing on the tomato paste, but a small offset spatula or the back of a spoon works well, too. Since the tomato paste is concentrated, a little delivers a lot of flavor. A thin layer also keeps the dough from sogging out after you add the toppings.

Roll the edge to make a raised rim if you'd like (or not). Don't fret about not filling the pan or having a perfectly round shape. It's more important that you avoid handling the dough too much.

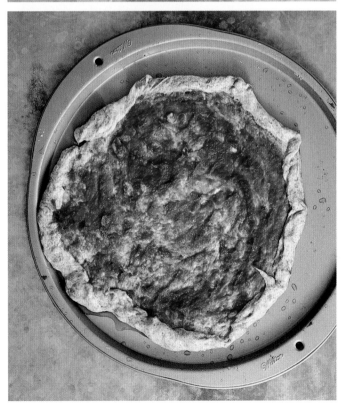

8. Smear dabs of sauce across the top of the pizzas with your fingers, pressing gently to keep the dough thin. (It's okay if the tops aren't fully covered.) Working in batches if necessary, bake on the lower rack until the bottoms of the pizzas brown in the sizzling oil and the tops darken and feel firm, 5 to 10 minutes for small pizzas or 10 to 15 for large; repeat as necessary. Transfer the pizzas to a wire rack. If you're not using a stone, return the baking sheets to the oven to keep them hot. At this point you can proceed or let the pizzas rest, loosely covered, for up to 2 hours. Remember to reheat the oven before you get back to work.

9. Top the pizzas with a little more of the tomato sauce if the tops look dry in spots; reserve any leftover sauce for another use. Scatter on the cheese and any toppings and, working in batches if necessary, return the pizzas to the oven, this time directly on the hot stone or baking sheets. Bake until the cheese is bubbly and the crust browns in places, 5 to 10 minutes. Put the pizzas back on the wire rack to set for a couple of minutes, then transfer to a cutting board, cut into wedges or squares, and serve.

Baked and Broiled Pizzas

We love finishing them like this. Make sure there's an oven rack close to the broiler element. After just a couple of minutes of the second bake in Step 9, remove the pizzas from the oven and turn on the broiler to high. Broil the pizzas just long enough to char the edges and brown the cheese in places.

Make This Deep-Dish Pizza on a Weeknight

You can take the same dough as the main recipe and adjust the timing to get a thick focaccia-like pizza that's different from the main pizzas but equally good. It's perfect for a workday schedule—or any time you won't be home to babysit the usual process.

All but one of the ingredients and quantities on page 142 remain the same: Instead of simmering your own thick sauce, use 170 to 225 grams tomato paste (one 6- to 8-ounce can or jar, or about 1½ tubes). Stir in 15 grams olive oil and 1 clove minced garlic if you like. Make this sauce up to a day ahead and keep it refrigerated until you're ready to bake the pizza.

THE NIGHT BEFORE

Before turning in the night before you want to eat pizza, combine the starter, 150 grams of the whole wheat flour, and 150 grams of the water in a large bowl to make the jumpstarter. Stir, scraping the sides and bottom as necessary, until all the flour is absorbed. Cover with plastic or a damp kitchen towel and let it sit at room temperature for 8 to 12 hours. The jumpstarter will bubble and become quite fragrant. Meanwhile, feed the remaining starter as usual: Add 75 grams each whole wheat flour and water and stir or shake. Cover and return it to the refrigerator.

THE NEXT MORNING

Make the dough by adding the remaining 300 grams flour and 150 grams water to the jumpstarter. Stir with a rubber spatula or your wet hands until a dough forms and looks springy, 1 to 2 minutes. If there's still flour not incorporated around the bottom or edges of the bowl, stir in more water

5 grams (about a teaspoon) at a time as you work. The dough should be wet and shaggy but will form a loose ball. Now cover again, and pop the dough in the fridge to rest all day.

BEFORE DINNER

A couple hours before baking (or when you get home from work), take the dough out of the refrigerator. With wet hands, fold the salt into the dough, adding enough water to create a sheen on the surface without the dough losing its ability to hold a loose shape. Cover and let it sit at room temperature for at least 1 or up to 2 hours. Skip the folding in Step 4.

Make the tomato sauce as described above (or take it out of the fridge if you already made it). Get your other toppings ready (again, see page 138). Maybe make a salad.

TO BAKE

About 45 minutes before you want to eat, move the rack to the middle but leave oven off. Line a 13 x 9-inch metal baking pan or rimmed baking sheet with parchment paper (covering as much of the sides as you can); grease the parchment generously with oil. Stretch the dough as much as you can in the air with your hands, then press it into the prepared pan. Smear it with the tomato sauce and top with cheese and one or two other toppings (don't overload it).

Cover the pan tightly with foil, put in a cold oven, set the heat to 425°F, and bake 30 minutes. Remove the foil and lift a corner of the pizza with a spatula so you can slip out the parchment; continue to bake until the top is bubbly and the crust is crisp around the edges, 10 to 15 minutes more.

Remove from the oven and let the pizza sit in the pan for a couple of minutes to set. Use a spatula to slide it onto a cutting board. Cut into squares and serve.

Focaccia

Making focaccia is as easy as baking Bittman Bread. You decide whether you want the finished product round or square, bearing in mind that the smaller the pan, the thicker the bread will be. Double the recipe and it perfectly fits a 13 x 9-inch rimmed baking sheet or metal baking pan.

Like most of our breads, focaccia starts covered, in a cold oven. (That's how you get the airy crumb.) Removing the foil to finish baking is how you get the crisp top, bottom, and sides.

All that's left to decide on the toppings. The main recipe starts with the classic rosemary and coarse salt. A list of more ideas follows on page 155.

To make sandwiches, use a square pan, cut the cooled focaccia into four squares and split the tops from the bottoms with a fork.

Makes

1 square or round focaccia
(3 to 6 servings)

Time

8 to 12 hours for the jumpstarter

About 3 hours intermittent activity to mix and fold the dough

About 90 minutes to shape, rest, and bake the focaccia

INGREDIENTS

100 grams whole wheat starter

300 grams whole wheat flour, plus 50 grams for feeding the starter

210 grams water, plus 50 grams for feeding the starter and more as needed for folding

7 grams salt, or to taste

30 grams (about 2 tablespoons) good-quality olive oil, plus more for rubbing the rosemary and for drizzling

1 sprig fresh rosemary

Large pinch coarse (or flaky) sea salt

1. Combine the starter, 100 grams of the whole wheat flour, and 100 grams of the water in a large bowl to make the jumpstarter. Stir, scraping the sides and bottom as necessary, until all the flour is absorbed. Cover with plastic or a damp kitchen towel and let it sit at room temperature for 8 to 12 hours. The jumpstarter will bubble and become quite fragrant. (The timing is flexible to fit your schedule; see "Baking Bread on Any Schedule" on page 89.) Meanwhile, feed the remaining starter: Add 50 grams each whole wheat flour and water and stir or shake. Cover and return it to the refrigerator.

2. When you're ready to make the dough, add the remaining 200 grams flour and 110 grams water to the jumpstarter. Stir with a rubber spatula or your wet hands until a dough forms and looks springy, 1 to 2 minutes. If there's still flour not incorporated around the bottom or edges of the bowl, stir in more water 5 grams (about a teaspoon) at a time as you work. The dough should be wet and shaggy but will form a loose ball. Cover again and let it sit for about 1 hour.

3. With wet hands, fold the salt and 1 tablespoon of the oil into the dough, adding enough water to create a sheen on the surface without the dough losing its ability to hold a loose shape. Cover and let it sit about 30 minutes.

4. Proceed with the four folds as described on page 64, at 30-minute (or so) intervals. As you work, wet your hands and the dough with enough water so that the dough becomes smooth while still holding some shape. Sometime over the course of the folds, strip the leaves from the rosemary and chop them. Line an 8- or 9-inch square baking pan or 10-inch ovenproof skillet with two overlapping sheets

continued →

of parchment paper (see the photo on page 153). Press them into the bottom and crease them over the lip to keep them in place. Spread the bottom and sides of the parchment with 1 tablespoon of the oil.

5. After the fourth fold, wet your hands one final time. Put the dough in the prepared pan. Put a few drops oil in your hand and rub the rosemary leaves in your palms to coat them. Scatter them on top of the dough, then dimple the dough lightly with your fingertips. Be gentle; resist the urge to stretch and pull the dough. Drizzle the top with another 1 tablespoon or so of oil. Cover with plastic or a damp kitchen towel and let it sit until the dough puffs a bit and an indent made with your finger springs back slowly, 15 to 30 minutes. Just before baking, sprinkle the top with sea salt if you like.

6. Cover the pan tightly with foil, put it in a cold oven, and set the heat to 425°F. After 15 minutes, carefully remove the foil. Continue baking until the top and sides are golden and crisp and an instant-read thermometer inserted into the center registers 200° to 205°F, 20 to 30 minutes. Transfer the bread to a wire rack and peel off the parchment. Let it cool a bit. Serve warm or at room temperature.

(opposite) Preparing the dough for baking: Dimples are quintessential focaccia. All the better for trapping olive oil, salt, and other toppings. With this whole wheat version, they also help the loaf rise evenly in the oven as it heats.

continued →

7 Ways to Top Focaccia

The idea is to scatter a wee bit of extra flavor on top. Remember, this isn't pizza!

1. A handful of seedless (or seeded) grapes of any color; halve them if they're big

2. Ditto cherry or grape tomatoes

3. Instead of the rosemary, try fresh lavender, oregano, mint, parsley, or dill

4. A few pitted olives, any kind; crushed with the flat side of a knife is best

5. Several anchovies, draped across the top

6. Chiles, either dried flakes or chopped fresh

7. A dusting of spice like curry or chili powder, or smoked or sweet paprika

American Muffins

No offense to our friends across the pond, but after tasting our incredible adaptation, Kerri's husband, Sean, claimed these flavorful whole wheat buns for America. The traditional stovetop cooking method delivers light English muffin–style rolls. They're intentionally ever-so-slightly underdone inside so that they're perfect after fork-splitting and toasting— tender and moist inside with a crunchy crust and lots of nooks and crannies.

Makes
6 large or 8 small muffins

Time
8 to 12 hours for the jumpstarter

About 3 hours intermittent activity to mix and fold the dough

About 30 minutes to shape and cook the muffins

continued →

INGREDIENTS

**100 grams whole wheat
starter**

**300 grams whole wheat
flour, plus 50 grams for
feeding the starter and
more for shaping the
muffins**

**210 grams water, plus
50 grams for feeding the
starter and more as needed
for folding**

7 grams salt, or to taste

**Medium-grind cornmeal
for dusting and cooking**

1. Combine the starter, 100 grams of the whole wheat flour, and 100 grams of the water in a large bowl to make the jumpstarter. Stir, scraping the sides and bottom as necessary, until all the flour is absorbed. Cover with plastic or a damp kitchen towel and let it sit at room temperature for 8 to 12 hours. The jumpstarter will bubble and become quite fragrant. (The timing is flexible to fit your schedule; see "Baking Bread on Any Schedule" on page 89.) Meanwhile, feed the remaining starter: Add 50 grams each whole wheat flour and water and stir or shake. Cover and return it to the refrigerator.

2. To finish the dough, add the remaining 200 grams flour and 110 grams water to the jumpstarter. Stir with a rubber spatula or your wet hands until a dough forms and looks springy, 1 to 2 minutes. If there's still flour not incorporated around the bottom or edges of the bowl, stir in more water 5 grams (about a teaspoon) at a time as you work. The dough should be sticky but easily form a fairly tight ball. Cover again and let it sit for about 1 hour.

3. With wet hands, fold the salt into the dough, adding enough water to create a sheen on the surface without the dough losing its ability to hold some shape. Cover and let it sit about 30 minutes.

4. Proceed with the four folds as described on page 64, at 30-minute (or so) intervals. As you work, wet your hands and the dough with just enough water so that the dough becomes smooth while still holding some shape. Again, don't add too much more water to the dough.

continued →

Medium-low and slow: Use more cornmeal than you think you should; a thin layer—rather than just a sprinkle—helps insulate the muffins and conduct heat during pan-cooking. And when we say "rotate" in the directions, we mean you keep the muffins on the same side, lift them with a spatula or fork, and spin them clockwise or counterclockwise to promote even browning.

5. After the fourth fold, spread a generous layer of cornmeal on a work surface. Divide the dough into 8 equal pieces for small muffins (about 75 grams each) or 6 pieces for large (about 105 grams each). Dampen your hands and gently roll each piece into a ball, then flatten it into a disk ¾ inch thick. Put it on the cornmeal. (You can put the muffins on a cornmeal-dusted plate, cover, and let them rest in the refrigerator for up to several hours; return them to room temperature before proceeding.)

6. When you're ready to cook the muffins, sprinkle the skillet or griddle with a generous layer of cornmeal and put the muffins in the pan, top side down; turn the heat to medium-low. (It's okay if the pan is crowded, but if you're more comfortable, work in batches; see the photo on page 159.) Cook undisturbed, adjusting the heat so the muffins release steam without scorching the cornmeal, until they're firm enough to move, about 5 minutes. After that, slip a spatula underneath and rotate them once on the same side to promote even browning, then let them cook for another 5 minutes or so. Flip the muffins and cook the other sides the same way, continuing to rotate and flip the muffins until they puff and cook evenly, another couple of minutes. Total cooking time will be 15 to 25 minutes.

7. The muffins are ready when they're firm to the touch but still slightly underdone inside; an instant-read thermometer inserted sideways should register about 180°F. Transfer the muffins to a wire rack. Let cool completely, then brush off the excess cornmeal. They'll keep, wrapped in a towel, for a day or so at room temperature, or refrigerated in parchment in an airtight container for up to a week. To serve, split the muffins by working a fork around the outside rim and breaking the muffins apart for toasting. (If you slice with a knife you won't get those terrific nooks and crannies.)

To split the muffins for toasting: Poke a fork in and out all the way around the edge then jiggle it to separate the two halves. Cutting with a knife won't give you the same nooks and crannies.

Garlicky Dinner Rolls

You can easily turn the basic Bittman Bread formula into all sorts of dinner rolls—like these garlic-stuffed puffs—and even hamburger buns. One simple process gives you many, many options, and we've even included a variation for a basic pull-apart. Rolls, of course, take more attention to shape than a single loaf, but they bake faster. If you don't have a standard-size muffin tin—with 8 to 12 cups—then make the Crescent Rolls or Pull-Aparts variation.

Makes

8 dinner rolls (or 4, 6, or 8 burger buns)

Time

8 to 12 hours for the jumpstarter

About 3 hours intermittent activity to mix and fold the dough

About 90 minutes to shape and bake the rolls

INGREDIENTS

100 grams whole wheat starter

300 grams whole wheat flour, plus 50 grams for feeding the starter

210 grams water, plus 50 grams for feeding the starter and more as needed for folding

7 grams salt, or to taste

4 large garlic cloves, peeled

50 grams olive oil (about a scant ¼ cup)

1. Combine the starter, 100 grams of the whole wheat flour, and 100 grams of the water in a large bowl to make the jumpstarter. Stir, scraping the sides and bottom as necessary, until all the flour is absorbed. Cover with plastic or a damp kitchen towel and let it sit at room temperature for 8 to 12 hours. The jumpstarter will bubble and become quite fragrant. (The timing is flexible to fit your schedule; see "Baking Bread on Any Schedule" on page 89.) Meanwhile, feed the remaining starter: Add 50 grams each whole wheat flour and water and stir or shake. Cover and return it to the refrigerator.

continued →

Garlicky Dinner Rolls and Crescent Rolls

2. When you're ready to make the dough, add the remaining 200 grams flour and 110 grams water to the jumpstarter. Stir with a rubber spatula or your wet hands until a dough forms and looks springy, 1 to 2 minutes. If there's still flour not incorporated around the bottom or edges of the bowl, stir in more water 5 grams (about a teaspoon) at a time as you work. The dough should be wet and shaggy but will form a loose ball. Cover again and let it sit for about 1 hour.

3. With wet hands, fold the salt into the dough, adding enough water to create a sheen on the surface without the dough losing its ability to hold a loose shape. Cover and let it sit about 30 minutes.

4. Proceed with the four folds as described on page 64, at 30-minute (or so) intervals. As you work, wet your hands and the dough with enough water so that the dough becomes smooth while still holding some shape. After the third fold, use about half the oil to generously grease 8 cups of a standard-size muffin tin. Mince the garlic. Combine it with the remaining oil in a small bowl, mashing with a fork to form a thin paste.

5. After the fourth fold, wet a clean work surface with water and press the dough into a rectangle about 12 x 8 inches. Make sure to wet your hands as you work. Cut the dough in half lengthwise, then across four times to make eight sort-of squares. Drape each into a greased cup and stretch the corners outward a little. Drizzle the inside of each dough square with the garlic–olive oil paste; fold the corners of dough inward toward the center. Cover loosely and let the rolls sit until they puff a bit, 15 to 30 minutes.

continued →

(top) Pressed dough, ready for shaping: For the rolls baked in muffin tins and the crescents, press the dough out into a rectangle about 12 x 8 inches, and cut either 8 squares or triangles (or a combination).

(center) For the crescents: Roll the dough from the bottom of the triangle to the tip. Then you can either curve the ends a little to create a bow or leave them straight. As you can see the exact shape of the triangle hardly matters since the dough is so easy to stretch and shape.

(bottom) For filled rolls: Drape each square of dough into a greased muffin cup, add the garlic oil (or whatever variation) then fold in the corners to enclose without sealing.

6. Put the muffin tin in a cold oven and set the heat to 375°F. Bake until the rolls are golden on top and the bottoms and sides separate from the cups, 35 to 45 minutes. (An instant-read thermometer inserted into the thickest part of a few should register about 200°F.) Let the rolls cool in the pan for a couple of minutes before loosely wrapping them in a clean kitchen towel to stay warm; serve as soon as possible.

Buttery Dinner Rolls

The most basic version. Omit the garlic and, instead of the olive oil, melt 57 grams (½ stick) butter and use that for greasing the cups and drizzling in Step 5.

Parmesan Dinner Rolls

The garlic is optional. Grate 60 grams (about 2 ounces) Parmesan cheese. Use either olive oil or melted butter as described in the main recipe or first variation. Use half to grease the cups as usual and combine what remains with the cheese (and the garlic if you're using it). Use that to drizzle into the rolls in Step 5.

Crescent Rolls

Omit the garlic. Use melted butter instead of olive oil and increase the quantity to about 85 grams (¾ stick). Line a large baking sheet with parchment. After pressing the dough into the rectangle in Step 5, cut it into 8 long, skinny triangles (see the photo on page 165). Brush the top of the dough lightly with about half of the butter. Starting with the shortest side of each triangle and stretching the dough a little as you work, roll each piece into a tight crescent. Transfer to the prepared pan, spacing the rolls about 2 inches apart. Cover lightly and let the rolls sit until puffed a little, 15 to 30 minutes. Drizzle the remaining butter on the rolls. Put the pan in a cold oven and set the heat to 400°F. Bake until the crescents rise and brown, 25 to 35 minutes. (An instant-read thermometer inserted into the thickest part should register about 200°F.) Cool on the pan for a few minutes before transferring to a wire rack.

Simplest Pull-Aparts

Omit the garlic and oil. Line an ovenproof 10-inch skillet or square baking pan with parchment paper. After the fourth fold, in Step 5 divide the dough into 8 equal pieces. With wet hands, shape the pieces into balls. Put them in the parchment-lined pan, starting in the center and quickly working around the sides to fill the pan; they shouldn't quite touch but should be evenly spaced. Let them rest until slightly puffed, 15 to 30 minutes, then cover the pan with foil, transfer to a cold oven, set the heat to 350°F, and bake until an instant read thermometer inserted into the middle registers about 205°F, 25 to 30 minutes.

Burger Buns

Four-inch ring molds make the buns perfectly round, with a true hamburger bun look. If you don't have them, you can improvise foil rings or bake the buns free form; they'll just be flatter and spread a bit more into an irregular shape—a

continued →

little like ciabatta rolls. Omit the garlic. Line the bottom of a 9- by 13-inch baking pan (not glass) with a sheet of parchment and put 6 ring molds on the parchment if you're using them. In Step 5, after the fourth fold, instead of rolling and cutting the dough, divide it into 6 pieces (or 4 for large or 8 for slider-style buns). With wet hands roll each into a ball and transfer to the parchment or mold, keeping them as far apart as possible; press gently. Rest and bake as directed in the Pull-Aparts variation: small buns will take about 20 minutes, standard size about 25, and large about 30 minutes.

Seeded Rolls, Crescents, or Buns

Poppy, sesame, fennel, cumin, caraway, all fair game for the main recipe or any of the previous variations. Omit the garlic. After drizzling the rolls with the oil or butter or molding the buns, sprinkle the tops with a dusting of seeds.

Amazing Biscuits

You and your trusty starter can make light and fluffy whole grain biscuits reliably and easily. The timing is flexible: Start the evening before for breakfast or brunch biscuits, or begin in the morning for evening biscuits. In addition to cheese in the second variation, other additions might include 2 teaspoons freshly cracked black pepper, 1 tablespoon chopped fresh rosemary or thyme, or 2 teaspoons curry or chili powder. And you can definitely use the biscuits to make berry or peach shortcakes, topped with whipped cream of course. (In this recipe and a couple of others, we use volume measures for the leavenings and salt because they are so small.)

Makes

8 biscuits (4 servings)

Time

8 to 12 hours for the jumpstarter

About 1 hour to mix, cut, and bake the biscuits

continued →

INGREDIENTS

**100 grams whole wheat
starter**

**120 grams buttermilk, plus
more if needed**

**220 grams whole wheat
flour, plus 50 grams for
feeding the starter**

**50 grams water for feeding
the starter**

**85 grams (¾ stick) cold
butter**

1 teaspoon baking powder

1 teaspoon baking soda

1 teaspoon salt

1. Combine the starter, buttermilk, and 100 grams of the whole wheat flour in a large bowl to make the jumpstarter. Stir, scraping the sides and bottom as necessary, until all the flour is absorbed. Cover with plastic or a damp kitchen towel and let it sit at room temperature for 8 to 12 hours. The jumpstarter will bubble and become quite fragrant. (The timing is flexible to fit your schedule; see "Baking Bread on Any Schedule" on page 89.) Meanwhile, feed the remaining starter: Add 50 grams each whole wheat flour and water and stir or shake. Cover and return it to the refrigerator.

2. Heat the oven to 450°F. Cut the butter into small bits, spread the pieces on a plate, and put the plate in the freezer to chill for 10 minutes.

3. Combine the remaining 120 grams flour with the baking powder, baking soda, and salt in another bowl. Rub the butter into flour mixture with your hands until it looks like streusel topping; put the bowl in the freezer for 5 minutes.

4. Add the chilled butter-flour mixture to the jumpstarter and stir gently with wet hands until the dough just comes together. It will be streaky but that's preferable to overworking the flour. If the dough doesn't come together easily, fold in more buttermilk, 1 teaspoon at a time.

5. Wet your hands again. If your bowl is broad enough, leave the dough where it is; or transfer it to a wet cutting board or work surface. Gently fold the dough once or twice and press it into a circle or rectangle about 1 inch thick. Cut the dough into circles with a biscuit cutter dipped in water (or for squares, use a small knife dipped in water). Gather the

continued →

scraps into a ball, press to 1 inch thick, and repeat until all the dough is used.

6. With wet hands, transfer the biscuits to an ungreased baking sheet, spacing them a couple of inches apart. Bake until browned on the top and bottom and firm to the touch, 10 to 15 minutes. Transfer to a wire rack. Eat them warm or within a couple of hours.

Amazing Drop Biscuits

These are faster to make, and scone-like. In Step 5, use a large spoon to drop the dough onto the baking sheet in 8 mounds. Bake as directed in Step 6.

Amazing Cheddar Biscuits

Works for either the main recipe or the previous variation. Fold in 100 grams grated cheddar cheese in Step 4 after adding the butter-flour mixture to the jumpstarter.

(clockwise, from top left)
The flour mixture should have visible bits of butter when you combine it with the fermented dough.

The two different components of the dough come together easily with wet hands, so you shouldn't have to overwork or knead it. You can either cut the biscuits in the mixing bowl or transfer the dough to a clean surface dampened with water.

To finish cutting the biscuits, simply gather the dough back together; try to avoid kneading or rolling. You'll get more height and flakiness with less handling.

Soft Pretzels

We hope the how-to photos here encourage you to try these truly special snacks, which are boiled (like bagels) before you pop them in the oven. (See "Twist and Shout" on page 179 for some other shaping options.) The cooking liquid is loaded with baking soda and sweetened with barley malt syrup to seal the dough and promote browning. Follow the directions for mixing the simmering brine carefully; it's a tad volatile. The dough contains less water than most of the other breads in the book, so it's easier to shape. For us, serving the pretzels with mustard is a must; which type is a matter of taste.

Makes

6 large pretzels

Time

8 to 12 hours for the jumpstarter

About 3 hours intermittent activity to mix and fold the dough

About 1 hour to shape, rest, boil, and bake the pretzels

INGREDIENTS

100 grams whole wheat starter

300 grams whole wheat flour, plus 50 grams for feeding the starter

180 grams water, plus 50 grams for feeding the starter and more as needed for folding and for boiling the pretzels

7 grams salt

55 grams (about ½ stick) butter, melted, or good-quality vegetable oil for greasing

44 grams barley malt syrup or 22 grams turbinado sugar

80 grams baking soda

1 egg

Coarse sea salt for sprinkling

Mustard for serving (optional)

1. Combine the starter, 100 grams of the whole wheat flour, and 100 grams of the water in a large bowl to make the jumpstarter. Stir, scraping the sides and bottom as necessary, until all the flour is absorbed. Cover with plastic or a damp kitchen towel and let it sit at room temperature for 8 to 12 hours. The jumpstarter will bubble and become quite fragrant. (The timing is flexible to fit your schedule; see "Baking Bread on Any Schedule" on page 89.) Meanwhile, feed the remaining starter: Add 50 grams each whole wheat flour and water and stir or shake. Cover and return it to the refrigerator.

2. To finish the dough, add the remaining 200 grams flour and 80 grams water to the jumpstarter. Stir with a rubber spatula or your wet hands until a dough forms and looks springy, 1 to 2 minutes. If there's still flour not incorporated around the bottom or edges of the bowl, stir in more water 5 grams (about a teaspoon) at a time as you work but keep the dough on the dry side; it should be sticky but easily form a fairly tight ball. Cover again and let it sit for about 1 hour.

3. With wet hands, fold the salt into the dough, adding enough water to create a sheen on the surface without the dough losing its ability to hold some shape. Cover and let it sit about 30 minutes.

4. Proceed with the four folds as described on page 64, at 30-minute (or so) intervals. As you work, wet your hands and the dough with just enough water so that the dough becomes smooth while still holding some shape. Again, don't add too much more water to the dough.

continued →

5. After the fourth fold, grease a baking sheet with some of the butter or brush with oil. Put some water on a work surface and divide the dough into 6 balls. With wet hands, roll each ball into a rope about 16 inches long. Wet your hands again and twist each rope into a large pretzel (see the photos on page 178). If they tear, just press them together again; it's okay if they aren't perfect. As you work transfer the pretzels to the prepared baking sheet.

6. Cover the pretzels with plastic or a damp kitchen towel and let rest until they puff slightly, about 30 minutes. Meanwhile, heat the oven to 450°F and bring 8 cups water to a boil in a large pot. Grease a wire rack with some butter or brush it with oil. Adjust the water to a vigorous simmer and add the malt syrup or turbinado sugar. Carefully add the baking soda, 1 to 2 teaspoons (6 to 12 grams) at a time, stirring to dissolve between each addition. Expect the liquid to foam up considerably; if it looks like the pot will overflow, turn off the heat until the foam subsides. When all the baking soda is incorporated, adjust the heat so the water simmers steadily but not violently.

7. Working with one pretzel at a time, use a skimmer or other similar tool to transfer it, face up, to the simmering water. Cook until the shape is set and the dough looks a little dry, about 45 seconds on each side, then remove it with the skimmer and transfer it (again, face up) to the greased rack to drain. Repeat with the remaining pretzels. When they're all boiled, wipe the baking sheet and grease it again. Transfer the pretzels to the pan so they've got some elbow room. Beat the egg with 2 teaspoons water to make an egg wash. Brush it over the tops of the pretzels and sprinkle them with coarse salt.

continued →

(top) Roll the balls into 16-inch ropes: You want the ropes to be long enough to leave open holes after shaping, but thick enough so the pretzels are chewy.

(center) Twisting pretzels, left to right: Start with overlapping one end of the rope over the other, leaving an oval loop on top. Twist the ends once. Then stretch the loop on the sides gently and fold it over the twist; this is now the bottom of the pretzel (shown at right). Turn them over and press the ends down gently. (The side showing the twist will become the top of the pretzel.)

(bottom) Submerging the pretzels in the bubbling syrup–soda mixture: After boiling, the pretzels will darken and develop a slight crust. (On the rack one is face up, one is face down. Does it even matter? As long as you get egg wash and salt on one side before baking, we don't think so!)

8. Bake until the pretzels are deep gold and glossy, 15 to 20 minutes. Cool on a wire rack until you can handle them. Serve while still warm, with the mustard on the side if you like. (These will keep at room temperature in a paper bag or bread box for 1 day.)

TWIST AND SHOUT

For pretzel rolls, you can just leave the dough in balls after dividing it. Or stretch and roll them into ropes as described in Step 5 and make simple knots or twists: For knots, grab each end and tie as you would a piece of rope or your shoestring. For twists, fold each long rope in half and tightly wrap the two sides around each other. Press the two ends together. Boil and bake as directed; rolls will take a little longer to bake than pretzels, twists, or knots.

Skillet Flatbread

Think of roti, pita, or chapati—only slightly tangy and way more flavorful than those made with white flour. This dough is drier than most of the others in this book, dry enough so you can use flour and a rolling pin to flatten the dough. As you cook the breads quickly in a smoking-hot dry skillet, they'll bubble and char beautifully in places, leaving you with chewy flatbreads that are sturdy enough to wrap as sandwiches, cut into wedges, or tear and drag through thick dips and spreads. You can finish them by brushing with melted butter or olive oil or serve them plain with something deliciously saucy. Grillers are going to love the variation.

Makes

6 large or 8 medium flatbreads

Time

8 to 12 hours for the jumpstarter

About 3 hours intermittent activity to mix and fold the dough

45 to 60 minutes to shape, rest, and cook the flatbreads

continued →

INGREDIENTS

**100 grams whole wheat
starter**

**300 grams whole wheat
flour, plus 50 grams for
feeding the starter and
more as needed for shaping
and rolling the breads**

**210 grams water plus
50 grams for feeding the
starter and more as needed
for folding**

7 grams salt, or to taste

1. Combine the starter, 100 grams of the whole wheat flour, and 100 grams of the water in a large bowl to make the jumpstarter. Stir, scraping the sides and bottom as necessary, until all the flour is absorbed. Cover with plastic or a damp kitchen towel and let it sit at room temperature for 8 to 12 hours. The jumpstarter will bubble and become quite fragrant. (The timing is flexible to fit your schedule; see "Baking Bread on Any Schedule" on page 89.) Meanwhile, feed the remaining starter: Add 50 grams each whole wheat flour and water and stir or shake. Cover and return it to the refrigerator.

2. When you're ready to make the dough, add the remaining 200 grams flour and 110 grams water to the jumpstarter. Stir with a rubber spatula or your wet hands until a dough forms and looks springy, 1 to 2 minutes. If there's still flour not incorporated around the bottom or edges of the bowl, stir in more water 5 grams (about a teaspoon) at a time as you work. The dough should be wet and shaggy but will form a loose ball. Cover again and let it sit for about 1 hour.

3. With wet hands, fold the salt into the dough, adding enough water to create a sheen on the surface without the dough losing its ability to hold a loose shape. Cover and let it sit about 30 minutes.

4. Proceed with the four folds as described on page 64, at 30-minute (or so) intervals. As you work, wet your hands just enough to do the folds without the dough sticking, but avoid adding too much water since you'll want the dough to be stiff enough to roll into flatbreads. After the third fold, line a plate with a kitchen towel or foil, cut five pieces of parchment paper, about 8 inches square (or seven 6-inch squares if you're making smaller breads). Prepare a work surface for rolling out the flatbreads; you'll want some extra flour handy.

5. After the fourth fold, divide the dough into 6 or 8 even pieces and dust your hands, the rolling pin, and the work surface with flour. Roll each piece out to a roundish or oval disk, no more than ¼ inch thick. Try to use only enough flour to prevent sticking without drying the dough out. As you work, move the flatbreads to a flour-dusted work surface or sheet of parchment; if you must stack them, layer the parchment squares between the disks. Let the dough sit until it puffs slightly, about 30 minutes. Or stack on a plate between flour-dusted sheets of parchment, cover, and refrigerate for up to a couple of hours.

6. Put a dry skillet or skillets, or a griddle, over medium-high heat. Working in batches to avoid crowding, put the flatbreads in the pan and cook, undisturbed, until they brown and release easily from the pan, about 3 minutes. Turn and cook on the other side, which usually only takes another minute or 2. As they finish, stack the flatbreads on the prepared plate and wrap them loosely. Serve as soon as possible. Or heat the oven to 200°F, loosely wrap the breads in foil, and put the packet directly on a rack for up to 30 minutes to keep warm.

Grilled Flatbread

After the third fold in Step 4, start the coals or heat a gas grill for hot direct grilling. Make sure the grates are clean. Working in batches if necessary, in Step 6 put the flatbreads on the grill directly over the fire. Quickly close the lid and cook until lightly browned on the bottom, with charring from the grates, 3 to 5 minutes. Turn and cook until browned on the other side and steaming, another minute or so. Transfer to the prepared plate. Repeat with the remaining flatbreads and serve as soon as possible.

Scallion Pancake

Turning your starter into a batter not only opens up a world of savory pancakes but makes this the easiest recipe in the book. Everyone can find something to love here: We always gravitate toward anything made with chickpea flour; both the scallion and kimchi versions are amazing; and we were astonished by the blini-ness of the buckwheat pancake.

Whichever direction you take, control the texture by making the batter thick enough to plop from a spoon (for crisp pancakes), or by making it soupy (for custardy pancakes). Use a 12-inch skillet for a pancake about ¼ inch thick; you can use smaller or larger pans instead to create a thicker or thinner pancake (adjust the baking time accordingly using the cues in the directions).

Makes

4 side dish or 8 appetizer servings

Time

6 to 12 hours to ferment the batter

1 hour to bake the pancake

GO DIRECTLY FROM STARTER TO SAVORY PANCAKE

Our longtime colleague Daniel Meyer cuts to the chase and uses starter as the batter for his pancakes. After adding enough water to make it spoonable, he fries it on the stove in a thin film of hot oil or melted butter. And if you want to add stuff—he suggests slightly crunchy cooked quinoa, for example—you can fold up to 40 percent whatever into 60 percent starter. Other add-in ideas include garlic, chopped apples, or spices.

continued →

INGREDIENTS

**100 grams whole wheat
starter**

**200 grams whole wheat
flour, plus 50 grams for
feeding the starter**

**300 grams water, plus
50 grams for feeding the
starter and more as needed
for adjusting consistency**

7 grams salt

1 bunch scallions

**50 grams good-quality
vegetable oil (about a scant
¼ cup)**

1. Combine the starter, whole wheat flour, and 300 grams water in a large bowl and stir until combined. The batter won't be smooth but should plop from the spoon or spatula. How much more water you eventually add will depend on how wet your starter is and your desired texture (see the headnote), but wait to see how the batter develops as it sits before you add more. Cover with plastic or a damp kitchen towel. Let the batter sit at room temperature for at least 6 or up to 12 hours. (The timing is flexible to fit your schedule; see "Baking Bread on Any Schedule" on page 89.) Meanwhile, feed the remaining starter: Add 50 grams each whole wheat flour and water and stir or shake. Cover and return it to the refrigerator.

2. Add the salt to the batter and whisk until it's smooth, adding water a little at a time until it's the consistency of thick pancake batter (for a thinner, crisper pancake) or thin pancake batter (for a thicker, more custardy pancake).

3. When you're ready to bake, heat the oven to 450°F. Slice the scallions into 1-inch pieces (at a diagonal is prettiest). When the oven is hot, put the oil in a 12-inch skillet and put the pan in the oven. Bake, checking frequently, until the oil shimmers without smoking, 3 to 5 minutes. Carefully remove the pan from the oven, scatter the scallions into the hot oil, and spread them out across the bottom of the pan. Using a circular motion, pour in the batter and swirl it into the hot oil with a fork like you're marbling cake batter.

4. Return the pan to the oven and bake undisturbed until the edges and top brown and the pancake releases easily from the pan, 30 to 35 minutes. Remove from the oven, slide the pancake out onto a cutting board, cut into wedges or squares, and serve.

Leek Pancake

Instead of the scallions, trim 1 medium-size leek to use the white and light green parts; halve it lengthwise. Cut the halves crosswise into crescents. Rinse well in a colander, drain well, and proceed with the recipe, cooking them in the oil in Step 3.

Shallot Pancake

Instead of the scallions, trim and peel 2 shallots and slice them thinly crosswise. Proceed with the recipe, using them in place of the scallions in Step 3.

Fresh Chile Pancake

Trim 1 or 2 hot red or green chiles (like jalapeño or serrano); seed them if you want the pancake less spicy. Slice them thinly crosswise and proceed with the recipe, using them in place of (or in addition to) the scallions in Step 3.

Chickpea Pancake

Tangier and a tad more breadlike than a traditional socca: Use the scallions in the main recipe, the shallots in the variation, or 1 small thinly sliced onion. Instead of the whole wheat flour, substitute besan (chickpea flour) in the batter.

continued →

Buckwheat Pancake

A springy flatbread that eats like blini. Omit the scallions and substitute 100 grams buckwheat flour for half of the whole wheat flour when you make the batter. Since the batter will be fairly thick, expect to add another 10 to 30 grams water in Step 3, depending on your desired texture. Everything else stays the same.

Corn Pancake

Think of a thin, crisp cornbread. Substitute medium or fine cornmeal for the whole wheat flour in the batter. If you like, instead of the scallions, add the kernels cut from 1 ear corn, or about ¾ cup frozen. Everything else stays the same.

Kimchi Pancake

Substitute brown rice flour for the whole wheat flour in the batter. Substitute up to 100 grams chopped kimchi (about ¾ cup) for the scallions.

Smaller Savory Pancakes

It's easy to turn the main recipe or any of the variations into pancakes of any size. Work on the stove instead of the oven and cook the vegetables in the hot oil over medium-high heat until they sizzle, then stir them, plus the oil in the pan, into the batter. Cook as the pancakes described on page 186.

Savory Hand Pies with Spinach and Feta

If you've made any of the other recipes in this book, by now you've probably noticed that our super-elastic and stretchy dough makes almost anything possible, even stuffed bread. Handling these little pies is a dream come true: They press easily into rounds, seal securely, and tears are easily mended simply by pinching. The main recipe is calzone-like, only with spanakopita filling. We've got you started with a few variations, but try these once and your own ideas will come easily. Hint: They're also terrific for using leftovers.

Makes

4 main dish or 8 to 12 appetizer servings

Time

8 to 12 hours for the jumpstarter

About 3 hours intermittent activity to mix and fold the dough and make the filling

About 1 hour to shape and bake the pies

continued →

INGREDIENTS

125 grams whole wheat starter

375 grams whole wheat flour, plus 65 grams for feeding the starter

250 grams water, plus 65 grams for feeding the starter and more as needed for folding

9 grams salt, plus more for the spinach

60 grams olive oil (about ¼ cup), plus more for drizzling

1 bunch scallions

4 cloves garlic

285 grams (about 10 ounces) fresh spinach

Pepper

170 grams (about 6 ounces) feta cheese

1 egg

Tomato sauce or full-fat yogurt for serving (optional)

1. Combine the starter, 125 grams of the whole wheat flour, and 125 grams of the water in a large bowl to make the jumpstarter. Stir, scraping the sides and bottom as necessary, until all the flour is absorbed. Cover with plastic or a damp kitchen towel and let it sit at room temperature for 8 to 12 hours. The jumpstarter will bubble and become quite fragrant. (The timing is flexible to fit your schedule; see "Baking Bread on Any Schedule" on page 89.) Meanwhile, feed the remaining starter: Add 65 grams each whole wheat flour and water and stir or shake. Cover and return it to the refrigerator.

2. When you're ready to make the dough, add the remaining 250 grams flour and 125 grams water to the jumpstarter. Stir with a rubber spatula or your wet hands until a dough forms and looks springy, 1 to 2 minutes. If there's still flour not incorporated around the bottom or edges of the bowl, stir in more water 5 grams (about a teaspoon) at a time as you work. The dough should be wet and shaggy but will form a loose ball. Cover again and let it sit for about 1 hour.

3. With wet hands, fold the salt into the dough, adding enough water to create a sheen on the surface without the dough losing its ability to hold a loose shape. Cover and let it sit about 30 minutes.

4. Proceed with the four folds as described on page 64, at 30-minute (or so) intervals. As you work, wet your hands and the dough with enough water so it becomes smooth while still holding some shape. After the third fold, prepare the filling: Chop the scallions and garlic. Put half of the oil in a large pot over medium heat. When it's hot, add the scallions and garlic. Cook, stirring occasionally, until soft,

continued →

about 3 minutes. Transfer to a bowl, return the pot to the stovetop, and raise the heat to high. Put the spinach in the pot, sprinkle with a little salt (the feta will add some to the filling too) and pepper, and cook, stirring constantly, until tender; transfer to a colander in the sink to drain and cool.

5. When the spinach is cool enough to handle, squeeze and press with your hands to release as much water as possible. Transfer the spinach to a cutting board and chop it. Add it to the scallions in the bowl. Crumble in the feta cheese. Mix, then taste and adjust the seasoning. Crack in the egg and stir with a fork to combine.

6. Heat the oven to 425°F. Grease a large baking sheet with the remaining oil. With wet hands, divide the dough into 4 equal pieces, or 8 or 12 for appetizer hand pies. Roll each into a ball and set them on the baking sheet or a wet work surface. Wet your hands again and, using your fingertips, gently press a piece of dough into a circle about 8 inches in diameter for full size (4 inches for appetizer size). Mound one-quarter (or one-eighth) of the filling over half, leaving a border of 1 inch at the edge. Fold the dough to enclose the filling, stretching it a little if necessary. Roll the edges of dough over a couple of times (again stretching a little), and seal by pressing the roll firmly with your fingers. Repeat with the other dough balls.

7. When all the hand pies are filled and sealed, cut three small slashes in the top of each to vent steam. Drizzle the tops with a little more oil. Bake until browned on the bottom and the top crust is golden and firm, 20 to 25 minutes. Serve hot or warm with tomato sauce or yogurt if you like.

continued →

The right stuffing texture:
Make sure you squeeze out the spinach so the filling isn't too mushy or wet. You can use all sorts of fillings inside these hand pies, just make sure to drain any extra fat, sauce, or liquid well before using.

Filling and sealing the hand pies:

(top) To avoid over-handling the dough—and to minimize the tears—Kerri likes to press, stetch, fill, and seal each dough ball directly on the greased baking sheet.

(center) Leave an inch border so you have some extra dough to roll and seal the edges.

(bottom) They only need an inch or so space between them during baking. Remember to cut the vents or the filling will bust out the sides.

Savory Hand Pies with Arugula, Ricotta, and Parmesan

Substitute arugula for the spinach. Instead of the feta, mix together 125 grams ricotta (about ½ cup) and 60 grams grated Parmesan (about ⅔ cup). Everything else stays the same.

Black Pepper Hand Pies with Prosciutto and Mozzarella

Figure you'll need 170 grams (about 6 ounces) each thinly sliced prosciutto and fresh mozzarella cheese. When you add the salt to the dough in Step 2, include 10 grams black pepper (about 4 teaspoons). Reduce the olive oil to 30 grams (2 tablespoons) just for greasing the pan, plus enough for drizzling. Omit the scallions, garlic, spinach, feta, and egg; skip the directions for cooking the filling. After greasing the pan and dividing and pressing out the dough in Step 6, slice the prosciutto crosswise into thin ribbons; pat the cheese dry with a towel and slice thinly. Scatter the prosciutto over half of the dough, top with the cheese, and enclose and seal as described. Dimple the top lightly with damp fingers before cutting the vents in Step 7. Drizzle with some olive oil and bake. Start checking after 15 minutes.

Savory Hand Pies with Curried Potatoes

Make the filling after the second fold rather than waiting for the third. Substitute good-quality vegetable oil for the olive oil. When you cook the scallions and garlic in Step 4, add 1½ inches fresh ginger, peeled and chopped. When the aromatics are soft, add 13 grams curry powder (about 2 tablespoons); transfer to a bowl and add 100 grams plain

Greek-style yogurt (reduced fat is fine; about ½ cup). Omit the spinach, feta, and egg. Fill a pot halfway with cold tap water. Add 600 grams (about 20 ounces) Yukon gold potatoes and a big pinch salt and bring to a boil. Cook until the potatoes are quite tender, 20 to 30 minutes. Drain well and transfer to the bowl with the aromatics. Mash roughly, skins and all, stirring to combine everything. Taste and adjust the seasoning, and add a handful of chopped cilantro, parsley, or mint if you've got it. Use this mixture to fill the hand pies as described in Step 6, and bake as directed.

FREEZES AND REHEATS LIKE A DREAM

This is one time when it can be worth it to make extra to freeze: After baking and cooling, wrap each stuffed bread individually in foil, seal in an airtight container, and freeze for up to a couple months. To reheat, put foil packet(s) on a baking sheet, straight from the freezer, slide the pan into a cold oven, and set the heat to 350°F. Once the bread is steaming, about 30 minutes, open the packet(s) and crank up the oven to 400°F to crisp the dough, just a few more minutes. Almost as delish as the first time around!

Cinnamon Rolls, page 209

CHAPTER 6

SWEET STUFF

**Pancakes and waffles,
cinnamon rolls, beignets
(and other doughnutty things),
tortes, and cookies**

Chocolate Chunk Torte, page 220

WITH THE MAGIC OF NATURAL, slow-action fermentation, 100 percent whole wheat desserts are not only possible, they're wonderful. And they're also intriguingly different. Because of the natural flavor of whole wheat and the bit of sweetness present in the germ, most of these desserts use less sugar than their white-flour counterparts.

Our only cheat—if we must call it that—is to occasionally include a small amount of baking powder or baking soda for a little extra lift.

The chapter starts with pancakes and waffles—classic sourdough preparations—followed, in keeping with the breakfast theme, by cinnamon rolls baked in a skillet, and the least fussy and most delicious beignets you've ever tasted.

The torte is a master recipe in the truest sense: The variations show how to turn a rich cake studded with dark chocolate into others juicy with stone fruits; there's even a coconut spin. Crumby Cookies turn leftover bread—every last crumb of it—into a quick and easy snack or dessert (or, well, we like them for breakfast).

Baking Sweets with Sourdough

MB:

This chapter reminds me of a prejudice I've developed against the word "sourdough." Yes, naturally fermented starter is acidic, but that doesn't mean your bread will taste "sour" (nor will it cause your sweets to taste anything but sweet). We use starter in sweet recipes not to promote sourness but to help make the treats you love with 100 percent whole grain flour. It's time for us to do some debunking.

KC:

Yes. Our whole wheat starter, like all so-called sourdough starters, is acidic, although not overly so. That acidity is tamed by using whole wheat flour, since there is a range of savory and pleasantly bitter and sweet flavors in the germ and bran. And as we know from the bread recipes, time mellows the flavor, too: As the dough uses natural yeasts and bacteria to ferment, other characteristics become more prominent.

MB:

A lot of people think you need cut in some white flour to make whole grain desserts that are as springy and tender as we expect them to be. That's where the starter comes in. It can leaven and lighten dessert batters and doughs the same way it does bread. And if you start with a lighter whole grain flour—a softer white wheat as opposed to a harder red one, a subtle distinction that's easy enough to understand with experience and looking again at the section on page 34—your desserts will be even closer to what you think of as the original.

KC:

We've also found that a small amount of chemical leavening—baking soda or baking powder—adds to rise and lift. And since both are slightly alkaline, they balance the acidity of the starter. And then we use a judicious amount of sugar to tip the overall balance toward sweetness.

MB:

You can hardly say that sugar is "good for you," but there's a place for it.

KC:

Yeah, can't argue with that. We've also found that you don't need much sugar in non-white-flour desserts. And the turbinado or "raw" kind we call for here delivers a broader spectrum of sweetness, with nuances of caramel and molasses that work perfectly with the flavors of whole grains.

MB:

Don't take our word for it. Try something in this chapter. Pancakes are a good place to start, as are the cinnamon rolls. And those beignets are pretty awesome . . .

Pancakes

The jumpstarter technique translates perfectly to pancakes or waffles in the morning. You get things rolling before you go to bed. Unless you want breakfast for dinner, in which case you start in the morning.

A couple of technical notes about the cooking: Whole wheat requires you maintain a slightly lower temperature than you'd normally use to cook pancakes; this gives them time for maximum rise while ensuring the centers are cooked through and the outsides are perfectly browned. You can make them any size, but we like to keep them on the small side, which makes them easier to maneuver in the pan or on the griddle.

Makes	*Time*
12 hearty pancakes (4 servings)	8 to 12 hours for the jumpstarter
	Up to 24 hours hibernation (optional but helpful)
	1 to 2 hours to mix the batter and cook (depending on whether the jumpstarter hibernated)

continued →

INGREDIENTS

100 grams whole wheat starter

225 grams whole wheat flour, plus 50 grams for feeding the starter

300 grams whole milk, plus more if needed

50 grams water for feeding the starter

30 grams turbinado sugar (about 2 tablespoons)

1 teaspoon baking powder

Pinch salt

2 eggs

30 grams butter, melted (about 2 tablespoons), plus more for cooking and serving

Maple syrup for serving

1. Combine the starter, 100 grams of the whole wheat flour, and 100 grams of the milk in a large bowl to make the jumpstarter. Stir, scraping the sides and bottom as necessary, until all the flour is absorbed. Cover with plastic or a damp kitchen towel and let it sit at room temperature for 8 to 12 hours. The jumpstarter will bubble and become quite fragrant. Meanwhile, feed the remaining starter: Add 50 grams each whole wheat flour and water and stir or shake. Cover and return it to the refrigerator.

2. If you're not ready to cook when the jumpstarter is ready, cover and let it hibernate for up to 24 hours (see "Baking Bread on Any Schedule" on page 89). Allow about an hour for it to come to room temperature before proceeding.

3. When you're ready to make the pancakes, add the remaining 125 grams flour and 200 grams milk to the jumpstarter along with the sugar, baking powder, and salt. Stir just to combine, then add the eggs and melted butter and stir again more vigorously until almost smooth; some lumps are preferable to overmixing. Add a little more milk if the batter doesn't plop from the spoon easily. Cover and let the batter sit until bubbly, at least 30 minutes but no more than 2 hours.

4. Heat the oven to 200°F. Fit a wire rack into a baking sheet and set it in the oven. Heat a large griddle or skillet (preferably cast iron, carbon steel, or nonstick) over medium heat. When a couple of drops of water skid across the surface of the pan before evaporating, it's hot enough. Put a pat of butter on the griddle or in the skillet. When the butter stops foaming, ladle in enough batter to make pancakes about 4 inches across each. Spread the batter evenly as necessary; you want them about ¼ inch thick.

5. Cook, undisturbed, until the edges are set and bubbles appear in the center of the pancakes, 2 to 4 minutes. Adjust the heat as needed; you want there to be some sizzling without burning.

6. Carefully slip a spatula under a pancake and peek to see if it's brown on the bottom; at this point you can rotate them on the same side to cook more evenly if you like. Once the bottom is brown, turn the pancakes. Cook the second side until lightly browned, another 2 to 3 minutes. Serve right away or transfer to the pan in the oven to keep them warm for up to 15 minutes while you cook the rest. Repeat with the remaining batter, adding more butter to the griddle as necessary. Pass maple syrup and more butter at the table.

Blueberry Pancakes or Waffles

You've really got to use fresh fruit here. Make either pancakes or waffles (page 206). Right before cooking, gently fold in about 250 grams (1 pint) blueberries, rinsed and well dried. Cook as directed.

Waffles

More work than pancakes (and also more butter!), but waffles are worth it. The results with starter make this whole wheat version spectacular. You can never go wrong with the usual maple syrup, though in the summer we like to serve the waffles with lightly sugared strawberries or other berries, or sliced peaches. And if you haven't tried waffles as a base for savory foods like smoked fish, braised vegetables or meat, or fried chicken (a classic), now is a good time.

INGREDIENTS

100 grams whole wheat starter

225 grams whole wheat flour, plus 50 grams for feeding the starter

300 grams whole milk

50 grams water for feeding the starter

30 grams turbinado sugar

1 teaspoon baking powder

Pinch salt

Good-quality vegetable oil for greasing the waffle iron

113 grams butter (1 stick), plus more for serving

2 eggs

Maple syrup for serving (or seasonal fruit; see the headnote)

Makes

8 round waffles (4 servings)

Time

8 to 12 hours for the jumpstarter

Up to 24 hours hibernation (optional but helpful)

1 to 2 hours to mix the batter and cook (depending on whether the jumpstarter hibernated)

1. Combine the starter, 100 grams of the whole wheat flour, and 100 grams of the milk in a large bowl to make the jumpstarter. Stir, scraping the sides and bottom as necessary, until all the flour is absorbed. Cover with plastic or a damp kitchen towel and let it sit at room temperature for 8 to 12 hours. The jumpstarter will bubble and become quite fragrant. Meanwhile, feed the remaining starter: Add 50 grams each whole wheat flour and water and stir or shake. Cover and return it to the refrigerator.

continued →

BITTMAN BREAD

2. If you're not ready to cook when the jumpstarter is ready, cover and let it hibernate for up to 24 hours (see "Baking Bread on Any Schedule" on page 89). Allow about an hour for it to come to room temperature before proceeding.

3. When you're ready to make the waffle batter, add the remaining 125 grams flour and 200 grams milk to the jumpstarter along with the sugar, baking powder, and salt. Cover and let the batter sit until bubbly, at least 30 minutes but no more than 2 hours.

4. Just before cooking the waffles, heat a waffle iron and brush it with a little good-quality vegetable oil if necessary. Heat the oven to 200°F. Fit a wire rack into a baking sheet and set it in the oven.

5. Melt the butter. Separate the eggs; add the yolks and melted butter to the batter and stir to combine. Beat the whites with an electric mixer or whisk until soft peaks form. Fold them into the batter with a rubber spatula. Try not to overmix; it's okay if there are streaks.

6. Ladle some batter into the hot waffle iron, careful not to overfill it. (If you want crisp edges, then purposefully underfill the iron; your waffles will look like the photo on page 207.) Close the iron and cook the waffles until they are browned and release easily, about 5 minutes, depending on your iron. Transfer to the prepared pan in the oven and repeat until all the batter is gone. Serve hot, passing more butter and toppings at the table.

Cinnamon Rolls

We put all the butter, sugar, and spice in the filling and crunchy topping so these little buns are a lot like eating the best cinnamon toast ever, but rolled up. You'll be shocked how easy the dough is to spread, fill, and roll—you don't even need a rolling pin.

For a nutty topping, scatter up to 50 grams chopped pecans or walnuts over the dough before adding the butter and sugar. And for a quick glaze, let the rolls cool a bit while you whisk together 227 grams confectioners' sugar with 60 grams milk; spoon that onto the warm rolls before serving.

Or do a 180 and check out the savory variations.

Makes

8 3-inch rolls (4 to 8 servings)

Time

8 to 12 hours for the jumpstarter

About 3 hours intermittent activity to mix and fold the dough

About 1½ hours to fill, roll, cut, rest, and bake the rolls

continued →

INGREDIENTS

100 grams whole wheat starter

300 grams whole wheat flour, plus 50 grams for feeding the starter

200 grams water, plus 50 grams for feeding the starter and more as needed for folding and pressing

7 grams salt, or to taste

113 grams (1 stick) butter, softened

75 grams turbinado sugar

10 grams cinnamon (about 4 teaspoons)

80 grams raisins (optional)

1. Combine the starter, 100 grams of the whole wheat flour, and 100 grams of the water in a large bowl to make the jumpstarter. Stir, scraping the sides and bottom as necessary, until all the flour is absorbed. Cover with plastic or a damp kitchen towel and let it sit at room temperature for 8 to 12 hours. The jumpstarter will bubble and become quite fragrant. (The timing is flexible to fit your schedule; see "Baking Bread on Any Schedule" on page 89.) Meanwhile, feed the remaining starter: Add 50 grams each whole wheat flour and water and stir or shake. Cover and return it to the refrigerator.

2. When you're ready to make the dough, add the remaining 200 grams flour and 100 grams water to the jumpstarter. Stir with a rubber spatula or your wet hands until a dough forms and looks springy, 1 to 2 minutes. If there's still flour not incorporated around the bottom or edges of the bowl, stir in more water 5 grams (about a teaspoon) at a time as you work. The dough should be wet and shaggy but will form a loose ball. Cover again and let it sit for about 1 hour.

3. With wet hands, fold the salt into the dough, adding enough water to create a sheen on the surface without the dough losing its ability to hold a loose shape. Cover and let it sit about 30 minutes.

4. Proceed with the four folds as described on page 64, at 30-minute (or so) intervals. As you work, wet your hands and the dough with enough water so it becomes smooth while still holding some shape. After the third fold, make the filling: Mash 85 grams (¾ stick) of the butter in a small bowl with 50 grams of the sugar and the cinnamon.

continued →

5. After the fourth fold, line a 10-inch cast-iron skillet, springform pan, or baking dish with a sheet of parchment paper that's big enough to overhang the rim by a few inches; press it into the bottom and crease the edges over the lip to keep it in place. Turn the dough onto a wet work surface and use wet hands to press it into a rectangle no more than ½ inch thick, about 14 x 9 inches, with the longer side toward you. (See the photos on the opposite page.) Dab the top evenly with bits of the cinnamon mixture. (Don't try to spread it or you'll tear the dough!) If you're using the raisins, scatter them evenly on top. Working from the long side closest to you, gently stretch and roll the dough tightly to enclose the filling. Set the log seam side down and cut it crosswise into 8 rolls. Put them in the pan so the spirals face up, fitting them in against each other and tucking in the seams. Cover and let the rolls rest until they puff slightly and an indent made with your finger springs back slowly, 15 to 30 minutes.

6. Dab the tops with the remaining 28 grams butter and sprinkle with the remaining 25 grams sugar. Cover the pan with foil, put it in a cold oven, and set the heat to 400°F. Remove the foil after 30 minutes and continue baking until the tops form a golden crust and the filling is bubbling, 15 to 20 minutes more; an instant-read thermometer inserted into the thickest bready part should register 200°F. Let the rolls cool in the pan a few minutes, then lift them out by the parchment. Serve warm.

continued →

(top) Press and fill: The dough easily presses into a thin rectangle on a damp surface. Then scatter the filling on top, leaving a border to allow for squishing during rolling.

(center) Roll: The log should be tight enough to hold together but loose enough to allow the dough to rise and expand in the oven.

(bottom) Slice and pan: These cinnamon rolls are pretty wet, so after cutting you just scooch them around on the paper without worrying too much about placement. Whether you use a round or square pan, they're going to touch. That's part of the plan.

Cardamom Rolls

Instead of cinnamon, use 5 grams cardamom (about 2 teaspoons). Add the grated zest of 1 orange to the filling in Step 4. Everything else stays the same.

Olive Rolls

Omit the sugar. For the filling in Step 4, instead of the butter, use 50 grams olive oil. Pit and chop 100 grams kalamata olives; you should have about ½ packed cup. Put them in a small bowl with the olive oil and add 2 cloves garlic, minced, the grated zest of 1 lemon, and lots of black pepper (no salt!). Mash with a fork until a paste forms. Proceed with the recipe from Step 5, drizzling the top of the rolls with a little extra olive oil instead of the butter and sugar as described in Step 6. Baking stays the same.

Herb Pinwheels

Ideal for people with herb gardens, since a mix of a few takes these rolls over the top. Omit the sugar. For the filling in Step 4, instead of the butter, use 50 grams olive oil. Chop some herb leaves—somewhere between 2 tablespoons and 1 cup; how much you use will depend on whether they're strong (like rosemary) or relatively mild (like basil, chives, or parsley). Put them in a small bowl with the olive oil and add 2 cloves minced garlic the grated zest of 1 lemon, and a pinch salt. Mash with a fork until a paste forms. Proceed with the recipe from Step 5, drizzling the tops of the rolls with a little extra olive oil instead of the butter and sugar as described in Step 6. Baking stays the same.

Drop Beignets

Mark literally stirred these up one morning on a whim, and they're now a staple—easy doughnut-like fritters you just drop into hot fat. A blizzard of confectioners' sugar is the New Orleans way to garnish beignets, applied when they're still hot to lay down a glaze; then dusted again on the plate. They're best eaten warm, but reheat well loosely wrapped in foil in a 350°F oven—even after being in the fridge a day or two. A candy or deep-fry thermometer is handy here to maintain the oil at the best temperature.

Makes

About 24 beignets (4 to 6 servings)

Time

8 to 12 hours for the jumpstarter

Up to 24 hours hibernation (optional but helpful)

2 to 4 hours to mix and ferment the batter (depending on whether the jumpstarter hibernated)

30 minutes to fry the beignets

continued →

INGREDIENTS

100 grams whole wheat starter

200 grams whole wheat flour, plus 50 grams for feeding the starter and more if needed to adjust the batter texture

100 grams water, plus 50 grams for feeding the starter

100 grams whole milk, plus more if needed

80 grams turbinado sugar

1 egg

Pinch salt

Good-quality vegetable oil for deep-frying (usually about a quart)

Confectioners' sugar for dusting

1. Combine the starter with 100 grams of the whole wheat flour and 100 grams water in a large bowl to make the jumpstarter. Stir with a rubber spatula or big spoon until the jumpstarter comes together in a loose dough or a thick batter; no traces of dry flour should be seen. Cover the bowl with plastic or a damp kitchen towel and let it sit at room temperature overnight, anywhere from 8 to 12 hours. (You can refrigerate the jumpstarter after fermenting to let it hibernate for up to 24 hours; let it come to room temperature before proceeding.) Meanwhile, feed the remaining starter: Add 50 grams each whole wheat flour and water and stir or shake. Cover and return it to the refrigerator.

2. Add the remaining 100 grams flour, the milk, turbinado sugar, egg, and salt to the jumpstarter; stir until smooth. The mixture should be somewhere between pancake and cookie batter. If it's too loose, add more flour 7 grams (1 tablespoon) at a time; if too thick, add more milk a little at a time. Cover and let the batter ferment at room temperature until bubbly, 2 to 3 hours.

3. When you're ready to cook, put 2 to 3 inches oil in a large, deep pot over medium heat; bring it to 350°F. Keep an eye on the pot; if it starts to smoke, turn off the heat immediately and resume when it's cooled down. Fit a wire rack into a large baking sheet.

4. Working in batches to avoid overcrowding, carefully use 1 or 2 tablespoons to drop a few beignets into the oil. (Scoop with one spoon and scrape with the other. Or use your finger to scrape.) Cook until the bottoms are deep golden,

continued →

about 3 minutes, then turn them with a slotted spoon. Cook until colored all over and cooked all the way through (an instant-read thermometer inserted in the thickest part should register about 200°F), another 2 to 3 minutes. As they finish, use the slotted spoon to transfer the beignets to the prepared rack. Repeat with the remaining batter, adjusting the heat as needed to keep the oil at 350°F.

5. Let the beignets sit for a couple of minutes to cool a bit, then dust with at least one layer of confectioners' sugar. Serve as soon as possible.

Cinnamon-Sugar Drop Doughnuts

Prepare the main recipe as directed. On a plate, combine 100 grams granulated sugar with 2 teaspoons (4 grams) cinnamon. After frying, drain the beignets briefly. Instead of dusting them with confectioners' sugar, carefully roll them in the cinnamon sugar while they're still warm.

Fruit Fritters

Makes 16 to 20 palm-size fritters. Works best with apples, peaches, nectarines, plums, apricots, and relatively firm pears. Weigh about 500 grams whole fruit (just over a pound); peel if you prefer, then trim, seed, or pit, and cut into slices or chunks no bigger than 1 inch. After the batter has fermented in Step 2, gently fold in the fruit until just incorporated. Keep the frying oil between 325° and 350°F and drop large spoonfuls of batter and fruit into the hot oil. Fry as described in Step 5, increasing the total cooking time to about 10 minutes. Kerri likes to dust these with cinnamon-spiked confectioners' sugar.

Cheese Puffs

These are like gougères, only with sourdough batter instead of choux pastry. You can go classic with Gruyère cheese, or use an aged cheddar, Parmesan, or manchego—or a combination. Mark especially likes to spike the batter with some black pepper and a small pinch of nutmeg. Omit the sugars. Just before frying, add up to 100 grams grated cheese to the batter.

Chocolate Chunk Torte

Naturally fermented cake with chopped chocolate is an unexpected treat. But all the flavor notes come together: The bitterness and coffee-ish taste of the dark chocolate, the subtle tang of the starter, and the caramelized sweetness of turbinado sugar combine to create a sophisticated and incredible cake.

The fruit versions in the variations make a show-stopping brunch centerpiece; begin the jumpstarter the evening beforehand. For dessert after dinner, pull things together in the morning. Creaming the butter and sugar forms the backbone of the batter, so don't skimp on that step; it helps to enrich and lighten the texture of the cake. And one final tip: If you want to serve the cake on a plate instead of right out of the pan, use a springform pan.

Makes

1 9-inch round or square cake
(8 servings)

Time

8 to 12 hours for the jumpstarter

15 minutes to mix the batter

50 to 60 minutes to bake the cake

continued →

INGREDIENTS

100 grams whole wheat starter

250 grams whole wheat flour, plus 50 grams for feeding the starter

125 grams whole milk, plus more if needed

50 grams water for feeding the starter

113 grams (1 stick) butter, plus more for greasing the pan

200 grams (about 7 ounces) dark chocolate

1 teaspoon baking powder

¼ teaspoon salt

150 grams turbinado sugar

2 eggs

1 teaspoon vanilla extract

Ice cream or whipped cream for serving

1. Combine the starter with 100 grams of the whole wheat flour and the milk in a bowl to make the jumpstarter. Stir with a rubber spatula or big spoon until the jumpstarter comes together in a loose dough or a thick batter; no traces of dry flour should be seen. Cover the bowl with plastic or a damp kitchen towel and let it sit at room temperature overnight, anywhere from 8 to 12 hours. (You can refrigerate the jumpstarter after fermenting to hibernate for up to 24 hours; let it come to room temperature before proceeding.) Meanwhile, feed the remaining starter: Add 50 grams each whole wheat flour and water and stir or shake. Cover and return it to the refrigerator.

2. An hour before you're ready to bake, take the butter out of the fridge to soften. Chop the chocolate into ½-inch chunks. Grease a 9-inch deep-dish pie plate, square baking pan or baking dish, or 9-inch springform pan with extra butter. Combine the remaining 150 grams flour with the baking powder and salt in a small bowl.

3. Heat the oven to 350°F. Put the stick of butter in a large bowl with the sugar and beat with an electric mixer or whisk vigorously until fluffy, 2 to 3 minutes (the sugar won't dissolve). Beat or whisk in the eggs one at a time. Beat or whisk until creamy, 2 to 3 minutes. Beat or whisk in the vanilla. (It's okay if the sugar isn't completely dissolved.)

4. Fold in the jumpstarter and the flour mixture with a rubber spatula or big spoon until just combined. Stir in the chocolate chunks. The batter will be a little stiff but not quite as firm as cookie dough; add a little more milk if necessary.

5. Spoon the batter into the prepared pan and bake until a toothpick inserted in the center comes out clean, 50 to 60 minutes. Cool in the pan on a wire rack. Serve warm or at room temperature, with ice cream or whipped cream. (Cover any leftover cake to store at room temperature and eat within a day, or refrigerate for up to 2 days.)

Berry Torte

Blueberries, raspberries, halved strawberries, blackberries, boysenberries, marionberries—you get the idea. The juice from the berries means you need a little less moisture in the batter. Reduce the milk in the jumpstarter to 100 grams. Instead of the chocolate, fold in 250 to 300 grams any berries (that's about a pint depending on the berry). Everything else stays the same.

Coconut Milk Torte

A rich, not-too-sweet soaked cake, loaded with coconut. Use 175 grams full-fat canned coconut milk instead of cow's milk. (Refrigerate the remaining coconut milk for later use.) Replace the chocolate with 75 grams unsweetened shredded coconut; omit the vanilla. When the cake goes into the oven, put the reserved coconut milk in a small saucepan over medium-low heat; you should have about 200 grams. Add 20 to 30 grams turbinado sugar (depending on your taste) and cook without boiling, stirring occasionally, until the sugar dissolves and the milk thickens a little, about 10 minutes. When the cake comes out of the oven, poke it all over with a fork and pour the coconut milk on top while it's still hot. After the cake cools, keep it refrigerated.

continued →

Whole-Lemon Torte

One of Kerri's absolute favorites. You use everything but
the seeds, so thin-skinned, slightly sweet Meyer lemons are
best. Omit the chocolate. Trim the ends from two lemons
and cut the flesh away from the core in 3 or 4 chunks; remove
any remaining seeds. Chop the lemon into ¼-inch bits. Beat
them into the creamed butter and sugar mixture with the
vanilla in Step 3. Finish the cooled cake with a glaze: Whisk
1½ cups confectioners' sugar with a couple tablespoons milk
until smooth. The rest stays the same.

Cherry-Vanilla Torte

Omit the chocolate. Same as with the berry cake, the
juice from the cherries means you need a little less
moisture in the batter. Reduce the milk in the jumpstarter
to 100 grams. When you take out the butter in Step 2, halve
and pit 300 grams cherries. (You should have a little more
than 2 cups when you're done.) Fold in the cherries in place
of the chocolate. Increase the vanilla to 1½ teaspoons
(8 grams). The rest stays the same.

Plum Torte

Italian prune plums are excellent here, but any variety will
work fine. Same as with the berry and cherry cakes, the
juice from the plums means you need a little less moisture
in the batter. Reduce the milk in the jumpstarter to
100 grams. When you take out the butter in Step 2, halve
and pit 300 grams plums. (You should have a little more
than 2 cups when you're done.) Fold in the plums in place
of the chocolate. The rest remains the same.

Crumby Cookies

The book ends as it began, with a recipe that doesn't require a naturally fermented starter. Though there are plenty of ideas for how to use leftover bread on page 113, this one produces a unique batch of cookies, with an excellent balance of chewy, cakey, and crunchy textures. For a thinner, more fragile cookie, see the last variation, which works on any of the spins here. With either approach, they're so good that you may find yourself baking a loaf of bread just so you can make cookies, though it's easy enough to just save pieces of bread in an airtight container in the freezer until you have enough.

Use any leftover plain bread here—Bittman Bread, Baguette, Mark's Rye, Kerri's Sandwich Loaf, or even Rich Sandwich Bread. Fresh loaves work, though the texture of the cookies will be chewier. You can also use the same quantity of already made crumbs, as long as they're unseasoned and not fried. For a crumby cookie that truly crumbles, in Step 1 spread out the bread cubes on a rimmed baking sheet and pop them in the oven for a few minutes while it heats to dry them out a bit.

Makes

2 dozen cookies

Time

About 45 minutes with leftover Bittman Bread

continued →

INGREDIENTS

350 grams leftover Bittman Bread (page 55), including crusts

200 grams turbinado sugar

170 grams (1½ sticks) butter, softened

2 eggs

8 grams (1½ teaspoons) vanilla extract

50 grams whole wheat flour

1 teaspoon baking powder

¼ teaspoon salt

1. Heat the oven to 375°F. Adjust the racks so they're toward the middle of the oven with several inches in between. Cut the bread into cubes no bigger than 1 inch; you should have 5 packed cups. Put the bread cubes in a food processor with the sugar and let the machine run until the mixture looks like wet sand, 1 to 2 minutes.

2. Add the butter and let the machine run until the dough starts to form a loose ball around the blade, about a minute. Scrape down the sides of the work bowl with a rubber spatula and repeat. Add the eggs and vanilla and let the machine run for another minute, stopping once or twice to scrape the sides again.

3. Combine the flour, baking powder, and salt in a large bowl. Transfer the bread crumb mixture to the bowl and stir until a somewhat loose dough forms.

4. Drop the dough by heaping tablespoons onto large ungreased cookie sheets. Space them about an inch apart; you should have about 24 cookies. Press the mounds down gently with your finger to flatten them. Bake, switching the cookie sheets between racks and rotating them if necessary after about 10 minutes to promote even baking, until the cookies begin to brown around the edges and are slightly firm to the touch, 20 to 30 minutes. Transfer them to a wire rack to cool. They'll keep in an airtight container at room temperature for several days or frozen for weeks.

continued →

Peanutty Crumby Cookies

Reduce the butter to 1 stick and add 100 grams peanut butter to the food processor at the same time in Step 2. Everything else stays the same.

Crumby Oatmeal Cookies

Replace half the flour with rolled oats (not instant) and add 100 grams raisins or chopped dark chocolate (or a combination). Everything else stays the same. (If you use this variation for the delicate recipe below you can't overload it with heavy ingredients, so skip the raisins and/or chocolate.)

Crumby Coconut Cookies

Sort of like macaroons. Replace 50 grams of the butter with coconut oil. Add 1 egg white when you add the eggs in Step 2. Add 50 grams unsweetened shredded coconut with the dry ingredients in Step 3.

Delicate Crumby Cookies

A simple tweak to the main recipe or any of the variations and they become a cross between a florentine and a sable. Reduce the flour in Step 3 to 30 grams. Be sure to space the cookies a couple of inches apart when you spoon them onto the cookie sheet. Let the baked cookies sit on the pan for a couple of minutes before transferring them to wire racks to finish cooling.

Chocolate Chunk Crumby Cookies

When you mix the dough in Step 3, fold in 100 grams chopped dark chocolate (that's a 3.5-ounce bar).

LAST FED 9/25 8am

300g KERRI's STARTER

100% WHOLE WHEAT
"FRANKENSTARTER"

FROZEN, REANIMATED w/

Life of a starter: For the photo shoot, Kerri and the team labeled "Frankenstarter" (see page 94) to keep track of feedings. And yes, you can repurpose a takeout soup container into a home for your starter.

Index

Note: Page numbers in *italics* indicate illustrations.

Tunnels, 47
Turbinado sugar, 38, 201
Turkey, 3

V

Van Over, Charlie, 1

W

Waffles, 206, *207*, 208
    Blueberry, 205
Walnuts, 38, 80, 209
Washington State University
    Breadlab, 4, 37
Water
    adding, 43, 84, 96–97
    quality of, 37
Wax paper, 41

Webbing, 86, 97
Weight-to-volume
    conversions, 43
Wet-Bread Stuffing, 115
Wheat berries, cracked, 78
White bread, 3, 87
White flour, 32–34, 200
    substituting, 87
White sugar, 38
Whole grain bread, 2–4, 9
Whole grain flour, 2, 32–36,
    96–97, 200
Whole grains, 32
    storing, 38
Whole-Lemon Torte, 224
Williams Sonoma, 8

Y

Yeast, 2, 16, 33, 34, 37, 47
Yecora flour, 35
"Young" starters, 93